THE FOOD LOVER'S INTRODUCTION TO BRITAIN

GRUB STREET • LONDON

Published by Grub Street, The Basement, 10 Chivalry Road, London SW11 1HT in association with Food from Britain

Food from Britain is the government and industry funded body whose role is to promote British food and drink both in the UK and overseas. The organisation works with all sectors of the industry – from producer to retailer.

International offices operate in France, Germany, Belgium, Holland, Spain and North America.

Food from Britain would like to thank the chefs, restaurateurs and food producers for their enthusiasm and co-operation.

First UK impression 1992

Copyright © Text Food from Britain
Design Copyright © Grub Street 1992

British Library Cataloguing in Publication Data
The food lover's introduction to Britain
647.9541

ISBN 0 948817 526

Text compiled by Food Matters, 20 Luxemburg Gardens, Brook Green, London W6 7EA

Cover photograph by Tim Imrie
Colour illustrations by Claire Davies
Line illustrations by Madeleine David
Design by Christine Wood
Typesetting by Chapterhouse, The Cloisters, Halsall Lane, Formby, L37 3PX

FRANCES BISSELL

Frances Bissell is one of Britain's leading food and cookery writers. As well as being the author of a number of cookery books, she writes every Saturday in 'The Times' and contributes to magazines both in Britain and abroad.

Although she has been called "the best private cook in Britain", she has been guest cook at some of the world's leading hotels, including the Mandarin Oriental in Hong Kong. She has also travelled widely to promote British food, to Bogota in South America and to Manila in the Far East and will soon visit Sri Lanka to help organise and promote a British food festival there.

PHOTOGRAPHIC CREDITS
Landscape Only: Title page, 18, 26, 33, 35, 36, 40; Aviemore Photographic: 6, 11; Robert Estall: 9, 34, 58, 61, 71, 78, 81(t), 84; Reed Farmers Group: 14, 76; AA Photo Library: 16, 47, 48, 49, 50, 51, 64, 68, 74, 76, 81(b), 86, 88; Anthony Blake: 20, 42, 53, 54, 55, 56, 62, 63, 67, 75, 80, 85; Northern Ireland Tourist Board: 22, 23, 25; Taste of Wales 28; John Heseltine: 31, 63, 69, 72; A–Z Collection: 38; British Tourist Authority: 70.

CONTENTS

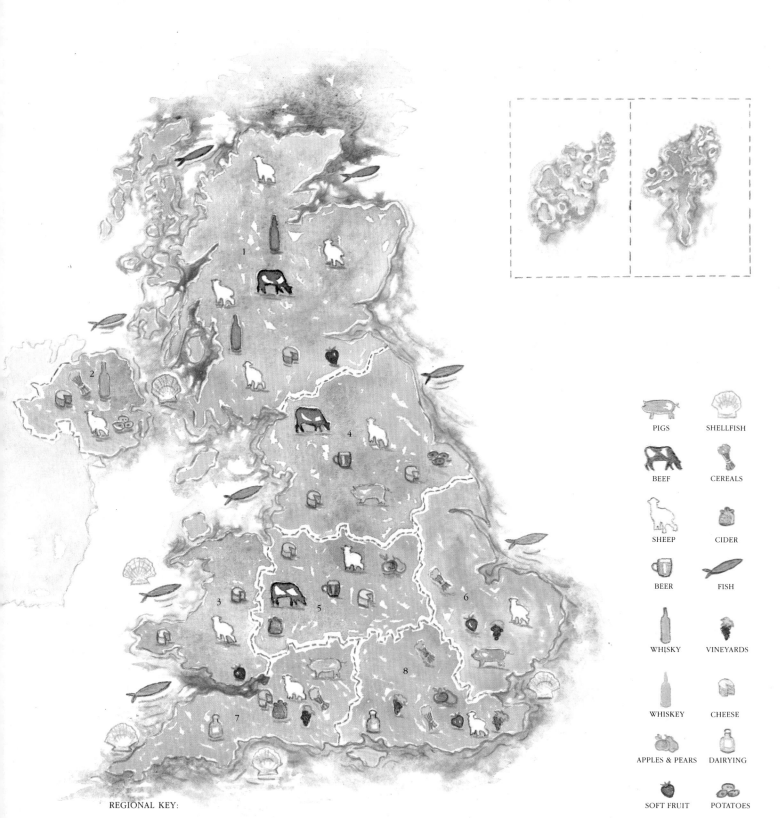

REGIONAL KEY:

1. SCOTLAND 2. NORTHERN IRELAND 3. WALES 4. NORTHERN ENGLAND

5. THE MIDLANDS 6. EAST ANGLIA 7. WEST OF ENGLAND 8. LONDON AND SOUTH-EAST ENGLAND

PIGS   SHELLFISH

BEEF   CEREALS

SHEEP   CIDER

BEER   FISH

WHISKY   VINEYARDS

WHISKEY   CHEESE

APPLES & PEARS   DAIRYING

SOFT FRUIT   POTATOES

FOREWORD

IN Britain we often complain about the weather, but it is this variable island climate and our geographical situation that we have to thank for the abundance and variety of produce that we enjoy year round. True, our asparagus season is brief, just three weeks in May and June. However, once East Anglia has yielded its green treasure, it is time to look to Kent, the Garden of England and its strawberry fields, soft fruit farms and cherry orchards. In high summer, our market stalls look like jeweller's display cases, row upon row of punnets piled high and overflowing with glowing ruby red currants, glossy jet black currants and even the rare pearly white currants. These luscious, intensely flavoured berry fruits make summer pudding, described on page X, a quintessentially English dish of great simplicity and elegance.

We do not have to look very far for the perfect companion to summer pudding. Devon and Cornwall, with their fertile green meadows, provide perfect pasture for dairy herds. Their rich milk in turn is used to make clotted cream, a rich buttery yellow thick cream which is quite unique and, like much of our cream, the envy of pastry cooks abroad.

Devon and Cornwall are also renowned for their specialist farmhouse cheeses but, in fact, all over Britain now, cheesemakers are returning to more traditional methods and recipes so that more and more regional cheeses are available. And at the right time of year, that is after the first frosts have crisped it up, nothing goes better with cheese than a head of sweet, nutty Fenland celery.

I find it difficult to write about food in the abstract and not in the context of a recipe or a meal, which is why here I seem to have started the meal backwards. But I do like to have my pudding last, in continental style, after the cheese. So let's bring on the main course. We do have a huge wealth of both recipes and ingredients to choose from. Is it to be a seasonal game dish? Perhaps a jugged hare in January or a brace of roast grouse from the Yorkshire Moors in August or September? Or a majestic haunch of venison from Scotland, served with rowanberry jelly, a vivid translucent red jelly made from the berries of the mountain ash? You might instead consider a dish of roast lamb, but will you choose the late born flavoursome hardy lamb from the Welsh hills or Scottish Highlands, or is it to be young spring lamb from Dorset? Our peculiar British mint sauce is not the only accompaniment to lamb. Try it with redcurrant jelly or roast it with a few sprigs of lavender. Perhaps you do not want a roast? The cheaper cuts of meat make up into beautiful dishes, succulent, comforting and with real depth of flavour, such dishes as oxtail, lamb stew or hot-pot, or steak, kidney and oyster pudding.

I have already mentioned summer pudding, but there is also our famous bread and butter pudding and the substantial steamed suet puddings, so good as winter desserts and now enjoying a well-deserved revival. These are homely, inexpensive dishes which waft enticing smells through the kitchen as they cook. And then there are the savoury puddings, like the steak and kidney made with suet for shortening, which is unbeatable for a light textured pastry which mops up the juices. It is an excellent vehicle for all kinds of ingredients. I particularly like to cook game puddings, using a mixture of, perhaps, hare and wild duck, or rabbit and pheasant.

The meat pie, however, is quite a different thing again from the pudding. Its origins go back well before the invention of the postal service and motorbike couriers to the days when our food, like ourselves, used to be transported by stage coach or horse and cart. A tasty meat mixture would be packed into a sturdy case of flour and water, a pie crust, wrapped and sent, say, from Bath to London where the meat would arrive in perfect condition. Nowadays, the pastry is perfectly good to eat, too.

Perhaps our richest harvest of all does not even come from the land, but from the sea and lochs which surround us. Langoustine, shrimps, freshwater crayfish, deep sea scallops, lobster and crab are found from Scotland to Cornwall and on the east and west coasts. Oysters, mussels and cockles come from the Thames estuary, the home of the famous native oyster, from the loughs of Northern Ireland and from the Gower peninsular in Wales, not to mention the Scottish lochs. And naturally enough, the different regions have traditional recipes, whether it's potted Morecambe Bay shrimps, buttered crab from Norfolk or oyster soup from the Gower. Rich fishing grounds provide us with herring and cod, salmon and sea trout in season. We have a long tradition of preserving fish, by curing and smoking, not only smoked salmon but the small haddock, smoked whole and eaten as they are, with bread and butter, known as Arbroath Smokies. There are few more appealing and simple starters to a meal.

This climate that we bemoan also gives us excellent potatoes, leeks, onions and other root vegetables, which have traditionally been cooked and served as not only accompaniments to our meat dishes but also as soups and dishes in their own right. They play an increasingly important role in our culinary heritage today, a heritage which is being honoured and renewed in kitchens up and down the country, not only in the professional chef's kitchen but also in the private cook's kitchen, as you will see from the recipes in this book. I hope you will enjoy them.

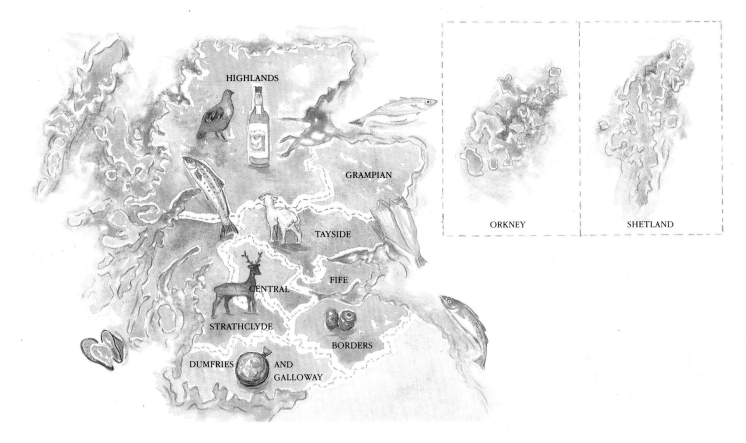

The labels on the map read:

HIGHLANDS

GRAMPIAN

TAYSIDE

FIFE

CENTRAL

STRATHCLYDE

BORDERS

DUMFRIES AND GALLOWAY

ORKNEY

SHETLAND

SCOTLAND

THE Scottish people have learned to make the most of the little which thrives in the country's bleakest regions. In the more mountainous northern reaches, grass grows thinly on the hard rock and the climate owes much to the Arctic, which shares the same latitude. Heavy rainfall and strong winds also combine to soak the valleys and ravines, nurturing only the sparsest of grass for the hardiest livestock to crop.

For centuries, much of Scotland existed through 'crofting'. Smallholdings based around peat-thatched dwellings dotted the moorlands and hillsides of most rural areas. Most food and drink was produced on the land, as each smallholding comprised strips of land growing oats, barley and root vegetables. In addition, there would usually be some livestock, such as Highland cattle, goats and sheep, grazing down from the mountains towards the sea.

The diet of the crofters was necessarily frugal although tasty and satisfying, made up of oatmeal-based dishes like porridge and oatcakes, mutton and salt fish, occasionally supplemented by freshly-caught luxuries like salmon and prawns. Each croft

The imposing edifice of Eilean Donan Castle rising up from Loch Duich on Scotland's West Coast

would house an open peat-burning fire over which food was cooked, with meat and fish hanging in the chimney to smoke.

Cows, goats and sheep were all used for their milk, as well as for skimmed-milk cheese.

Changes have swept across Scotland, however, especially with the arrival of North Sea Oil to its coastline and islands, and traditional crofting communities can now only be found in certain areas, such as the Inner and Outer Hebrides, Orkney, the Shetland Isles and parts of Ross & Cromarty and Sutherland.

Contrasting harshly with the frugal, almost monotonous diet of the crofting community of the Highlands and Islands, Scotland's aristocracy dined well on dishes using the best of local ingredients cooked to more sophisticated recipes. When Queen Victoria acquired Balmoral Castle in the 19th century, elaborate French-influenced English dishes were blended with traditional Scottish ones, allowing guests to taste the flavour of Scotland without offending their palates.

Scotland is currently enjoying a revival of interest in its food and drink, with numerous hotels and restaurants gaining international acclaim for their intelligent and creative use of Scottish ingredients. Many dishes which were once considered strictly for leaner days have been carefully embellished and added to gourmet menus, while prime Scottish beef, lamb, seafood and fruit have been pounced upon by chefs from all over the world eager to develop new ideas with traditional ingredients.

AIRDS HOTEL, Port Appin, Airds Bay, Argyll
Telephone: 063 173 236
The internationally-renowned Airds Hotel is situated on the eastern shore of Loch Linnhe, with breath-taking views across the loch to the Movern hills. Everything that is best about Scottish cooking is found at Airds – the finest local ingredients and wonderful hospitality in stunning surroundings.

SALMON AND DILL FLAN

PASTRY
8 oz/225 g/1½ cups plain flour
salt
2 oz/56 g/¼ cup butter
2 oz/56 g/¼ cup lard
2 fl oz/50 ml/3½ tbs cold water

FILLING
3 eggs, lightly whipped
½ pt/425 ml/1½ cups double cream
salt and pepper
grated nutmeg
1 lb/450 g raw salmon, chopped into small pieces
bunch of fresh dill

To make the pastry, rub the butter and lard in the flour until the mixture resembles fine breadcrumbs. Gradually add the cold water until the mixture binds together. Set aside in the fridge for 30 minutes.

Preheat oven to 200°C/400°F/Gas Mark 6. Line the greased flan ring with pastry, prick base, cover with greaseproof paper and baking beans. Place in the oven on the top shelf for 10 minutes. Remove paper, brush flan with beaten egg and put back in the oven for eight minutes until golden brown in colour.

Put the salmon pieces in cooled flan case. Pour in the whipped eggs and seasoning and sprinkle with sprigs of dill. Bake in a cool oven 170°C/325°F/Gas Mark 3 until set and slightly puffed.

Serves 4
(AIRDS HOTEL)

Two of Britain's busiest fishing ports are on the east coast of Scotland. ABERDEEN and PETERHEAD land large quantities of the country's favourite fish, including cod, haddock, whiting,

halibut, sole and mackerel. Although much of the catch is sent to Liverpool on the west coast and Billingsgate market in London, sea fish still forms a very important part of the Scottish diet, haddock and lemon sole being the most popular species. Indeed, fish vans still travel from coast to coast distributing fish to towns and villages, and fishmongers are able to offer the freshest fish due to the proximity of the fishing ports.

Herrings were once caught in huge quantities all around the Highland coast but EC fishing restrictions have affected the figures quite dramatically. Some dishes still survive, however, such as herrings in oatmeal, popular as it makes use of two local staples.

SOUSED HERRING WITH MUSTARD SAUCE

4 herrings
4 oz/110 g/¾ cup carrots
4 oz/110 g/¾ cup onion
1 bay leaf
6 peppercorns
¼ pt/150 ml/½ cup vinegar
salt and pepper

SAUCE
6 oz/125 g/1 cup natural yoghurt
2 oz/56 g/2 tbs grain mustard
juice of half a lemon

Heat the oven to 180°C/350°F/Gas Mark 4. Clean, scale and fillet the fish. Wash the fillets and season with salt and pepper. Roll up with the skin outside and place in a greased earthenware dish. Peel the carrot and onion and cut into neat thin rings. Add to the herring with the bay leaf, peppercorns and vinegar. Season with salt and pepper. Cover with greaseproof paper and cook in the oven for 15–20 minutes. Allow to cool, then place in a serving dish with pieces of lemon and parsley. Serve with the sauce.

To make the sauce, stir together the yoghurt, mustard and lemon juice.

Serves 4
(MURDO MACSWEEN AT OAKLEY COURT)

There are still areas of Scotland which enjoy thriving fishing industries, namely the Western Isles and Orkney. Here, where the islands deflect the warming waters of the Gulf Stream, fish and shellfish are caught in abundance. Lobster, crab, mussels, shrimps, cockles and scallops, as well as many varieties of white and flat fish have for centuries been caught in small vessels around the islands.

SEAFOOD SPECIALISTS OF ORKNEY, Cairston Road,
Stromness, Orkney
Telephone: 0856 74267
To arrange a visit to the various shellfish farmers and distributors
in Orkney, please telephone Remy Manson on the above number.

A group of seven seafood farmers and processors based in
Orkney, Seafood Specialists of Orkney have been trading as a
group since 1989. Orkney itself, six miles north of the Scottish
mainland, is surrounded by clean waters, rich in seafood and
relatively unpolluted. The members have now pooled their
resources in order to raise the profile of Orkney seafoods, while
at the same time providing top quality fresh products distributed
through an efficient and reliable service to the UK and Europe.

ORKNEY SMOKEHOUSE, Cairston Road, Stromness, Orkney
Telephone: 0856 850844
• Smoked shellfish

NORTH ISLES SHELLFISH, Hatston Industrial Estate, Kirkwall,
Orkney
Telephone: 0856 6161
• Fresh shellfish

BENESTHER SHELLFISH, Old Schoolhouse, Deerness, Orkney
Telephone: 0856 74267
• Farmed shellfish, prepared shellfish dishes

ORKNEY SALMON CO. LTD., Lambholm, Orkney
Telephone: 0856 78414
• Wild and farmed salmon, fresh and smoked

LANG-GEO OYSTERS, Lang-Geo, Finstown, Orkney
Telephone: 0856 76544
• Farmed shellfish

HEBRIDIAN SCALLOPS WITH WILD MUSHROOMS AND GLAYVA

½ oz/14 g/1 tbs butter
6 large fresh scallops
2 fl oz/60 ml/4 tbs fish stock
1 fl oz/30 ml/2 tbs white wine
2 fl oz/60 ml/4 tbs cream
Glayva, to taste
1 small carrot, finely cut into small strips
¼ of a small leek, finely sliced
½ oz/14 g/2 tsp chantrelle or oyster mushrooms
half a shallot, finely chopped
1 oz/28 g/1 tbs hazelnut butter
several sprigs of chervil
diced tomato

Melt the butter in a pan. Add the scallops, fish stock and
white wine and gently poach for 1–2 minutes. Remove the
scallops and keep warm. Reduce the liquid until syrupy. Add
the cream, Glayva, strips of carrot, leeks, mushrooms and
shallot and bring to the boil. Correct the seasoning, and stir in
the hazelnut butter. Finally, add the scallops. Serve
immediately and garnish with sprigs of chervil and diced
tomato. This could also be served as a first course in a small
puff pastry case.

Serves 2

(MURDO MACSWEEN AT OAKLEY COURT)

GLAYVA is a traditional Scottish liqueur made from a blend of
the country's best whiskies.

A significant spin-off of Scotland's long fishing tradition is its
smoking and curing. Largely due to the necessity to preserve
food for the long and cold winters, many traditional methods
have survived and remain unchanged in the remoter areas.
However, the regional cures, such as Finnan haddock and Loch
Fyne kippers, are recognised hundreds of miles away from their
original home.

The day's catch at Stornoway in the Western Isles

ARBROATH SMOKIES

In common with many curing methods, the Arbroath method of curing haddock has Norse origins. Small whole haddock are gutted and salted for around an hour, before being tied together in pairs. The salt is then washed away and the fish are hung across wooden bars to dry. When the skin is quite hard, the fish are smoked over slow hardwood fires for around 45 minutes, by which time they will have turned dark brown in colour. Arbroath smokies may be eaten hot or cold. The fishing village of Arbroath still contains rows of small smoking sheds where haddock are cured in this way. Demand is high both locally and nationally for this truly regional product.

R. R. SPINK & SONS, 13 High Street, Arbroath, Tayside
Telephone: 0241 73246
Fifth generation fishmongers, whose range includes locally caught wet fish as well as top quality Arbroath smokies.

FLAN OF ARBROATH SMOKIES

SAUCE

1 lemon
4 fl oz/110 ml/½ cup virgin olive oil
4 g/1 tbs caster sugar

FLAN

1 pair of Arbroath smokies, about 10 oz/285 g
3 eggs, size 3
3 fl oz/90 ml/6 tbs creme fraiche
juice of half a lemon
freshly ground pepper

GARNISH

6 oz/170 g/¾ cup cabbage, shredded
walnut oil
1 small carrot, peeled and shredded
1 small raw beetroot, peeled and shredded
1 oz/28 g/1 tbs pine kernels, toasted

To make the sauce, peel the lemon, carefully removing all the pith and membrane. Cut into segments, removing all the pips. Place the segments into a liquidiser and blend. Slowly add the olive oil, then add the sugar and blend until thickened.

Split the smokies in half, removing all the flesh from the skin. This is easier if they are warmed first in a moderate oven at 350°F/180°C/Gas Mark 4 for 10 minutes. Puree the flesh to a fine paste in a food processor. Add the eggs and blend briefly. Then add the cream fraiche and blend again until just mixed. Push the mixture through a fine mesh sieve. Add the lemon juice and season with black pepper.

Lightly butter 6, 3¼ in/8 cm ramekins. Divide the flan mixture between the ramekins. Stand them in a roasting tin half filled with water. Bring the water in the tin to the boil on top of the cooker. Cover with foil, then reduce heat to a simmer. Check after 7–8 minutes. The flan is cooked when the point of a knife inserted in the centre comes out clean. Before serving, gently saute the shredded cabbage in the walnut oil. Place a flan in the centre of each individual plates and garnish with shredded cabbage and the remaining vegetables. Sprinkle with a few pine kernels. Gently warm the sauce and pour over each flan. Serve immediately.

Serves 6

(DAVID WILSON, THE PEAT INN AT FIFE)

The rivers of Scotland are cold and fast-running and the lochs are deep and pure. Their waters contain some of the finest salmon and trout to be found anywhere in the world. The Rivers Tay, Tweed and Spey provide important revenue for Scotland, as commercial fishing becomes increasingly valuable. Wild salmon is officially fished from January through to November, although each river has its own specific season. Brown trout may be fished from March 15th to October 6th, while rainbow trout has no close season and may be fished all year.

Combining two Scottish traditions, SMOKED SALMON is one of the country's most famous products. There are hundreds of salmon smokers across Scotland, ranging from the small traditional family-run businesses to enormous mechanised operations. The Scottish Salmon Smokers' Association aims to highlight those smokers who produce an authentic, high quality product so that the consumer may be guided in his or her choice of smoked salmon. All its members use Atlantic salmon, either wild or farmed, which has been caught in Scotland and smoked over oak woodchips. A salt cure may be supplemented by a little sugar.

Fish farming has taken off in Scotland to an extent which other regions can only follow, with farmed trout and salmon supplementing supplies of wild fish, at much cheaper prices.

The SCOTTISH SALMON FARMERS' MARKETING BOARD will provide a list of salmon farmers in Scotland whose products reach high standards of quality and distribution. Information about Scottish farmed salmon, including quality assurance schemes and nutritional details may be obtained from the SCOTTISH SALMON INFORMATION SERVICE.

SCOTTISH SALMON FARMERS' MARKETING BOARD, Drummond House, Scott Street, Perth
Telephone: 0738 35420

SCOTTISH SALMON INFORMATION SERVICE, 26 Fitzroy Square, London W1
Telephone: 071 388 7421

Trout fishing at a fish farm near Aviemore

It is said that nowhere else in the world grows RASPBERRIES as perfectly flavoured as Scotland. Scotland itself certainly recognises the fact, establishing a thriving raspberry growing industry over a hundred years ago which provided two-thirds of the UK's requirements until relatively recently. Many large-scale operations now grow raspberries solely for jam-making and pureeing while others grow smaller quantities and offer surplus stock through Pick-Your-Own ventures.

RASPBERRY AND DRAMBUIE ICE CREAM

6 eggs
16 fl oz/425 ml/1 ½ cups double cream
2 fl oz/56 ml/4 tbs raspberry puree
juice of 1 large lemon
2 fl oz/56 ml/4 level tbs Drambuie
8 oz/225 g/1 cup caster sugar

Separate the eggs, putting the whites into one bowl and mix the yolks in another one. Mix together the raspberry puree, lemon juice and Drambuie. Put the cream in a bowl and whisk until it is firm, then gradually fold in the raspberry mixture gently. Whisk the whites until they form stiff peaks, and then whisk in the sugar a tablespoon at a time, until stiff, after each addition. Gently whisk in the yolks until evenly blended. Fold the cream into the egg mixture. Turn into a deep plastic container and freeze.

Serves 4–6

(AIRDS HOTEL)

SELECTED RASPBERRY GROWERS
Please telephone to make appointments to visit. The following raspberry growers generally only sell raspberries on a wholesale basis.

EASTER BALLINDEAN FARM, Inchture, Perth
Telephone: 0828 86256

GAGIE HOUSE FARM, Dundee, Angus
Telephone: 082 621 207

THOMAS THOMSON LTD., Keathbank, Blairgowrie, Perthshire
Telephone: 0250 2266

It is easy to see the influence OATS have had over Scottish cooking. Even today, when wheat is widely cultivated in the more fertile areas, dishes using oatmeal remain an important part of modern Scottish diets. Students at Edinburgh University are still allocated one day off a year, known as Meal Monday, to go home to collect a year's supply of oatmeal, although its original purpose is seldom remembered today.

Oats are still farmed in Scotland and are probably one of the most natural crops in Britain, requiring the least processing. There are five common forms into which oats are made:

1. *Groats*: the complete, whole-grain oat
2. *Jumbo Oats*: lightly-rolled oats, used for thick porridge
3. *Rolled Oats*: more finely-rolled oats, used for ordinary porridge
4. *Oatmeal*: cut, rather than rolled, oats, generally available in 3 grades
5. *Oat Flour*: the finest grade, for baking and thickening

Many Scottish soups and broths use oats for thickening, such as the ones listed below; and herrings and certain soft cheeses are often rolled in oatmeal to add texture.

Haggis: the most famous of all the Scottish specialities, haggis underwent numerous changes over the years to become the well-loved and widely available product it is today. The sheep's pluck (lungs, heart and liver) are combined with oatmeal, suet, onions, herbs and other seasonings, and boiled in a sheep's bag, or stomach. Haggis is traditionally served with mashed swede and potatoes and malt whisky.

Excellent Scottish haggis is available from the following suppliers:
JOHN A BELL, Islay, Argyll
Telephone 0496 84656

CASTLE MCLELLAN FOODS, Kirkcudbright, Dumfries & Galloway
Telephone: 0557 30905

DAVID A HALL, Broxburn, Edinburgh
Telephone: 0506 853300

MACBETH'S, Moray, Grampian
Telephone 0309 72254

MACSWEEN'S, Edinburgh
Telephone: 031 229 1216

JAMES MCINTYRE, Rothesay, Isle of Bute
Telephone: 0700 503672

JOHN SCOTT & SON, Dunfermline, Fife
Telephone: 0383 724337

STRATHMORE MEAT LTD., Forfar, Angus
Telephone: 0307 62333

Scotch Broth: Meat, together with pulses and vegetables, was originally simmered in a large cauldron over an open peat fire. It might be thickened with oatmeal or barley. If the meat was thought to be good enough, it was taken out when cooked and eaten as a meal in itself, the remaining soup being put aside for a separate meal. However, if the meat was of poor quality, the whole broth would be eaten at one sitting.

Cullen Skink: Another Scottish soup, originally an essential part of the crofting diet but now served in hotels and restaurants across the land. It is largely made up of smoked haddock, thickened with potatoes.

White Pudding/Mealie Pudding: White pudding actually exists in one form or another all over the world, anywhere where times have been hard. It contains no meat as such, just oatmeal, beef suet, onions and seasonings in a sausage-type casing.

The importance of oats is most obvious in Scotland's wide variety of bakery dishes, many of which are now made without oats but still remain hugely popular. Porridge, eaten all over the world during winter for breakfast, is still a Scottish favourite. Breakfast is also incomplete without a morning roll, a soft yeasted bap eaten warm and floured. Many traditional bakery products can be traced back to the days of baking on a griddle – bannocks, made with enriched oatmeal dough and eaten all over the country, are now delivered from the bakeries daily by bread vans.

The Scotch pie, again a dish recognised all over Britain, is made with a hot water crust and contains minced meat and gravy, a meal in itself. Another popular lunch-time dish is the Forfar bridie, steak, onion and gravy inside a shortcrust pasty, originating in the town of Forfar, just north of Dundee. Other towns have their own types of bridie.

The Scottish oatcake differs from others in that it is thinner, crisper and often larger and is frequently eaten with soft Scottish cheese. Tasty and healthy, oatcakes are now exported all over the world. Also well-known outside Scotland is Dundee cake, a rich and satisfying fruit cake. The region is also renowned for its shortbread, which in various shapes and sizes is distributed widely in America and Europe.

RECOMMENDED SUPPLIERS OF SCOTTISH BAKERY
PRODUCTS

G W GILLIES, 8 Park Street, Portknockie, Buckie, Banffshire
Telephone: 0542 40541
Gillies produce Scotch pies for sale from their shop and also on a
wholesale basis. Other products include Portknockie
gingerbread made to an old local recipe and a range of luxury ice
creams.

SIMMERS, Romano Lodge, 43 Station Road, Corstorphine,
Edinburgh
Telephone: 031 334 0852
Shortbread, biscuits and oatcakes are produced by Simmers, who
distribute their products throughout the UK. Traditional Scottish
cakes, made with malt whisky and Drambuie, are also available.

WALKERS SHORTBREAD LTD., Aberlour on Spey, Banffshire
Telephone: 03405 555
Walkers are probably most famous for their shortbread, instantly
recognisable all over the world in its tartan packaging. They also
produce oatcakes, cakes and biscuits and several catering
products.

SCOTTISH SHORTBREAD

¾ lb/340 g/2½ cups plain flour
½ lb/225 g/1 cup softened butter
¼ lb/110 g/½ cup granulated sugar
pinch of salt

Heat oven to 170°C/325°F/Gas Mark 3. Put all the ingredients
into the mixing bowl of an electric mixer and blend together
well. Roll out the mixture on a floured surface, approximately
¼ in/1 cm thick. Cut into rounds with a biscuit cutter. Prick
the top of the biscuits with a fork, then bake in the oven for
about ¾ hour or until pale in colour. Remove the tray from
the oven, then sprinkle the top of the biscuits with caster
sugar. Cool the biscuits on a wire rack. When cool, store in
an air tight container.

(THE PEAT INN AT FIFE)

The most famous Scottish cattle of all is the ABERDEEN ANGUS, a
breed developed from Highland cattle on the North East coast in
the early 19th century, although its predecessors can be traced
back to the Viking age. The Aberdeen Angus is a distinctive
beast, its heavy black body giving a high proportion of prime
cuts. The cattle are usually bred on the hills and uplands, then
brought down to the richer pastures for feeding and growing.

The flavour of MUTTON or LAMB obviously reflects the food
that the sheep has consumed. Black-faced lambs in Scotland's
hills and mountains graze on heather, which gives their meat a
sweet flavour. In the lower grounds of Northern Scotland and
the Borders, the fields are populated by Cheviot sheep, a
popular breed all over Britain. Of particular note are the hardy
Shetland sheep, living on the Scottish coastlands and cropping a
mixture of grass, heather and seaweed. The iodine in the
seaweed gives a gamey quality to their meat.

Most of rural Scotland is rich in GAME, its open moorlands,
heather-covered hills and mountain ranges providing the
perfect habitat. Each type of game has its own season when
parties are supposed to shoot, although rough-shooting and
poaching takes place most of the year.

BANDS OF PERTH, 135 Glover Street, Perth
Telephone: 0738 24222
For the past 50 years, Bands of Perth have been supplying the
best of Scotland's wild game to caterers, supermarkets and
individual consumers, recently branching out into the European
market. All game sold by Bands is guaranteed shot in Scotland and
the range is very impressive – red and roe deer, hare, rabbit,
wood pigeon, pheasant, native grey and red-legged partridge,
wild duck, grouse, woodcock and snipe.

The largest game to be stalked in Scotland is deer, which roam
wild in Highland forests more prolifically than anywhere else in
Britain. Roe deer are considered to be the best, followed by
fallow deer then red deer. Venison has been a popular Scottish
dish for centuries, the haunch and saddle being roasted while
the less tender cuts are stewed, braised and devilled. The meat
has a tendency to be quite dry, so it should be well larded before
cooking or marinaded for longer than normal.

Deer farms are becoming a valuable Scottish industry. There
are currently around 50 working deer farmers in Scotland, thus
increasing the availability of venison and many venison
products, such as sausages and haggis.

Game birds proliferate in Scotland, from the red grouse
whose shooting season begins on the 'Glorious 12th' – although
it is roasted with cranberry or rowanberry jelly right through to
mid-December – and its related capercaillie to the rare
ptarmigan, arguably too rare these days to shoot. Once rare but
now on the increase, native grey partridges are still shot from
1st September; their numbers were drastically decreased
through over-shooting during the 18th century, so red-legged
partridges, known as Frenchmen, were imported as a supplement.

In no danger of extinction is the pheasant, populating not
only the moors and field but also, to the motorist's despair, the
lonely country roads. The important factor to bear in mind
when deciding how long to hang pheasant is how it was shot
and the time of year. A clean shot bird should be hung for no
longer than a week. If the weather is frosty, however, it may be
hung for longer.

Deer farming is now one of Scotland's most valuable industries

SEASONS

GAME BIRDS	SEASON	EATING PERIOD	SCOTTISH DEER	SEASON
Pheasant	1 October–31 January	November–December	Red deer – Stag	1 July–20 October
Partridge	1 September–31 January	October–November	Red deer – Hinds	21 October–15 February
Grouse	12 August–10 December	August–December	Roe deer – Buck	1 May–20 October
Blackgame	20 August–10 December	September–October	Roe deer – Does	21 October–28/29 February
Capercaillie	1 October–31 January	September–November		
Ptarmigan	12 August–10 December	September–December		
*Woodcock	1 September–31 January	October–December		
Snipe	12 August–31 January	August–January		
Inland wildfowl	1 September–31 January	September–January		
Foreshore wildfowl	1 September–20 February	September–February		
Wild Geese	1 September–20 February	September–January		

Venison may be eaten at any time except during the close seasons.

* Scotland only – in England and Wales, the season for
  woodcock begins a month later.

CHEESES

CHEESE has been made on farms and in crofts throughout Scotland since the 13th century; the oldest cheese recorded in the world, Crowdie, was probably made around this time in the Highlands and Western Islands and was still being made in quantity until as recently as 1939.

During the 18th century, most Scottish cheeses were made with skimmed milk left over from butter-making and matured in ox bladders. Things progressed well for Scottish cheesemaking until the 1870s, when the Scottish Dairy Association adopted the Canadian Cheddar production method, which eradicated much of the traditional haphazardness, such a vital part of the cheeses' character. Scottish determination won through, however, with 300 farms still producing traditional Dunlop cheese in 1930. It was not until the outbreak of World War Two and the introduction of enforced block cheesemaking that Scottish cheeses went into serious decline. As recently as 1967, there were only six traditional cheesemakers left in Scotland. However, it would be true to say that there has now been something of a revival in Scottish cheesemaking, especially of some of the ancient varieties such as Caboc and Crowdie. There are also some new cheeses coming out of Scotland which are gaining excellent reputations all over the world, such as Bonchester and Dunsyre Blue.

CROWDIE

Originally produced in the crofting regions of the Highlands and Islands, Crowdie is a soft, low-fat crumbling cheese with a faint whisper of lemon in its flavour. It can be eaten on Scottish oatcakes or mixed with double cream and rolled in oatmeal and peppercorns – a blend known as Black Crowdie.

CABOC

Currently more popular in England than Scotland, Caboc is a soft curd cheese brought to Scotland in the 15th century by Mariota de Ile, the daughter of a Macdonald, Lord of the Isles.

DUNLOP

The first full-cream cheese to be made in Scotland was Dunlop, a hard cheese made with the milk of Ayrshire cattle. The original recipe was brought to the town of Dunlop around 1688 by a farmer's wife from Ireland who fled from the upheavals caused by King James II in her native country.

SCOTTISH (AND ORCADIAN) CHEESEMAKERS
Please telephone to make appointments to visit.

EASTER WEENS, Bonchester Bridge, Hawick, Roxburghshire
Telephone: 045 086635
- Bonchester – unpasteurised Jersey cow's milk cheese, full-fat soft, mould-ripened
- Teviotdale – unpasteurised Jersey cow's milk cheese, full-fat semi-hard

H J ERRINGTON & CO, Walston Braehead, Ogscastle, Carnwath, Lanarkshire
Telephone: 089 981 257
- Dunsyre Blue – unpasteurised cow's milk cheese, matured for 3 months
- Lanark Blue – mould-ripened, unpasteurised ewe's milk cheese

EXPRESS DAIRIES CREAMERY, Lockerbie, Dumfries & Galloway
Telephone: 0387 810771
- Dunlop – pasteurised hard cheese, matured for 7–8 months, not widely available but worth seeking out

HIGHLAND FINE CHEESES LTD., Blarliath, Tain, Ross & Cromarty
- Crowdie – unpasteurised, low fat
- Caboc – made with curd, double cream and oatmeal
- Galic – soft, full-fat, with garlic, oats and nuts

MICHAEL MARWICK, Walltower Farm, Howgate, Penicuik, Midlothian
Telephone: 0968 72263
- Crowdie – unpasteurised, low fat
- Langskaill – pressed, unpasteurised
- Lothian – soft, unpasteurised, matured
- Pentland – soft, unpasteurised, matured
- Smallholder – cow/goat's milk cheese, mould-ripened with maturation, unpasteurised

MICHAEL NEILSON, Windyknowe, Annan, Dumfries & Galloway
Telephone: 04612 4691
- Barac – unpasteurised Freisland ewe's milk cheese, full-fat, hard, matured for a minimum of 3 months
- Corban – unpasteurised Freisland ewe's milk cheese, soft, also available with chives

NORTH OF SCOTLAND MILK MARKETING BOARD, Kirkwall, Orkney
Telephone: 0856 2824
- Orkney – a modern version of Dunlop, available plain, coloured or smoked
- Claymore Crowdie – made with skimmed milk, soft

By the mid 18th century, Dunlop cheese had become so popular and demand so high that it replaced most of the cheese made from skimmed milk and many of the Scottish sheep's milk cheeses. Eventually, all farmers making cheese from Ayrshire cow's milk called their products Dunlop, until its quality became so varied that the Ayrshire Agricultural Association felt bound to step in. A thorough investigation resulted in improved production methods, as well as better hygeine standards and temperature control.

The people of Orkney refer to themselves as Orcadians and are more closely related to the Norse rather than the Scots, much Norse language surviving in their everyday speech. A wide variety of cheeses has been made in Orkney for centuries, dwindling only when beef cattle began to replace dairy herds. Orcadian cows, often one per household, still produce milk for cheese, under the strict control of EC regulations.

Nobody knows for sure when the Scots first began distilling malted barley to produce WHISKY. The Ancient Celts certainly enjoyed a busy distilling industry, calling the powerful brew ''uisge beatha'', the water of life, and Scotch whisky became renowned for its reviving and warming qualities, greatly appreciated in the Scottish climate.

The climate and the geography of Scotland are ideal for distilling. Plenty of rain and cool air, pure waters, soil suitable for barley-growing and huge areas of peat for burning all combine to produce excellent whisky.

Whisky was distilled for centuries in homes and farmhouses on a purely open and domestic level. Things changed, however, when the Scots Parliament brought in the Excise Act in 1644, taxing all production of whisky. This inevitably led to secret distilling operations and clandestine drinking houses, known as shabeens, tucked away in the crofting villages. Scotch whisky was also smuggled into the cities and towns, to avoid taxation.

By the mid 19th century, distilling had been completely legalised and the Scots were allowed to build the hugely successful industry which continues to thrive today, with over 100 distilleries. The Scots are justifiably proud of their unique product and have protected it from imitations by giving it a strict definition: whisky may only be called Scotch if it is distilled and matured in Scotland.

There are two types of Scotch whisky, malt and grain. Malt whisky may be produced from a single malt or a blend of malts, while grain whisky may be combined with various malts to produce a particular blend.

The production process for both malt and grain whiskies are more or less the same. Malted barley is steeped in water and yeast for 2 or 3 days before germinating. It is then spread out, often by hand, on the malting floor, to germinate.

Once germination is complete (each distiller will gauge this differently), the malted barley is dried in a kiln. Smoke filters up gently through the barley to dry it out. It is at this stage that peat is added, giving its special aroma to the barley and the final product its distinctive flavour.

Scotch whisky is Scotland's most valuable export. In 1979,

£707M worth of whisky was exported, increasing to £1469M in 1989. It is exported to 190 different foreign countries, with the USA, Japan and Australia taking the lion's share.

There is a handful of distilleries in Scotland which can be visited without making an appointment beforehand. Their opening times are restricted however.

GLENFIDDICH DISTILLERY, Dufftown, Banffshire
Open Monday to Friday 10.00 am to 12 noon, 2.00 pm to 4.30 pm.
From July to August open from 10.00 am to 12 noon every day.

THE GLENLIVET DISTILLERY, Glenlivet, Banffshire
Open from Easter to the end of October.
Monday to Friday, 10.00 am to 4.30 pm.

GLENFARCLAS, Marypark, Ballindalloch, Banffshire
Open all year, Monday to Friday, 9.00 am to 4.30 pm.

TAMDHU DISTILLERY, Knockando, Morayshire
Open from May to September, Monday to Friday, 10.00 am to 4.00 pm.

STRATHISLA-GLENLIVET DISTILLERY, Keith, Banffshire
Open from mid-June to August, Monday to Friday, 9.00 am to 4.00 pm.

CALEDONIAN CREAM

*½ pt/290 ml/1 cup double cream
1 oz/28 g/1 tbs orange marmalade
½ fl oz/14 ml/1 tbs lemon juice
2 oz/56 g/¼ cup caster sugar
1 fl oz/30 ml/2 tbs of The Glenlivet*

Whisk the cream until thick. Combine all other ingredients and gently fold in the cream. Spoon into individual pots and serve chilled.

Serves 2
(MURDO MACSWEEN AT OAKLEY COURT)

Casks of whisky maturing in the Glenfiddich Distillery at Dufftown

NORTHERN IRELAND

NORTHERN Ireland is a mild, fresh and moist land with pure clean waters, perfect for growing crops and breeding healthy animals. The rainfall is quite heavy, giving the grasslands an unrivalled lush greenness.

The beautiful landscape is varied, made up of hills, lakes, pastures and peaceful glens, with lakes of all sizes making up a vast proportion of the region. In fact, one third of Co. Fermanagh lies underwater. Consequently, Fermanagh's traditional ways of making a living were farming and fishing.

CO. ANTRIM, arguably one of the most beautiful regions in the whole of Ireland, is dotted with fishing villages nestled against the cliffs, a reminder of the days when merchants crossed the Giant's Causeway which separates Ireland from Scotland to trade with the Scots. Antrim is also home to much of Northern Ireland's largest freshwater lake, Lough Neagh, and the beautiful ruined castle of Dunluce.

The richest farmlands in Northern Ireland, as well as some of the country's best sea angling at the ports of Portavogie and Ardglass, are to be found in CO. DOWN.

To enjoy the best of the province's fresh ingredients and its legendary hospitality, Belfast is probably the best place to go. Whether you visit a large hotel restaurant or a small pub in a side street, you will be assured of one of the warmest welcomes in Britain.

ROSCOFF'S Shaftesbury Square, Belfast
Telephone 0232 331532 is one of the city's most renowned restaurants; Eugene Callaghan, Roscoff's Sous Chef, recently won the prestigious Roux Diners Scholarship for his deceptively simple use of local produce.

The country's chequered history is above all intrinsically linked to the POTATO. Ireland is the only country to have become wholly dependent on the potato during the 18th century, for

The beautiful rugged coast line of Co Antrim

A delicious selection of traditional home-baked breads

this crop is ideally suited to the land and climate.

Much of Ireland's tradition of potato and milk dishes is still found all over the province. Although poverty no longer makes it necessary to eat potato mashed with turnips or potato soup, they are still popular because, perhaps surprisingly, they taste rather good. Potatoes, known as 'murphys', are often cooked in their skins so that all the flavour is retained. They also feature in many bakery products, such as potato bread, pies and cakes.

Northern Ireland, perhaps more so than Southern Ireland, has a long tradition of home-baking which continues to thrive today. Bread is often baked at home using bicarbonate of soda and buttermilk as raising agents. Bread from the local bakeries is usually only bought as a supplement. There is a very wide range of breads enjoyed on a daily basis, including wheaten bread, potato bread, boxty bread and farls. Farls are simply triangular quarters of bread, which with lashings of Irish butter are utterly irresistible.

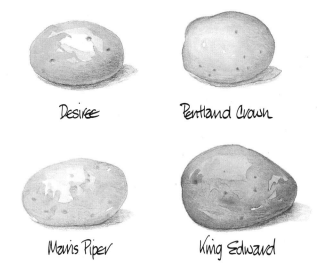

Desirée

Pentland Crown

Maris Piper

King Edward

IRISH SODA BREAD

1 lb/450 g/3 cups white flour
10 fl oz/300 ml/1¼ cups buttermilk
2 g/½ tsp baking soda
2 g/½ tsp salt

Heat the oven to 200°C/400°F/Gas Mark 6. Sift all the dry ingredients together into a bowl, make a well in the centre and add enough buttermilk to make a thick dough. Mix well with a wooden spoon, bringing in the flour from the sides to the centre. Add more milk if the mixture seems too stiff. Lift the mixture to a lightly floured board and knead lightly. Flatten the dough into a circle. Put onto a greased baking sheet, scoring the top with a floured knife in the form of a cross. Bake in the oven for about 40 minutes or until it makes a hollow sound when tapped.

(CONNIE O'MAHONEY)

As in Wales and Scotland, griddle baking still plays an important part in the region's cookery. Scones and biscuits which were originally baked over a hot griddle in farmhouses and village bakeries are still hugely popular at the all-important 'high tea'.

Thankfully, much of the Northern Irish seacoast is still relatively unpolluted. The people of the province have been harvesting from the seas for centuries. In the far north, near the Giant's Causeway, herrings and mackerel were almost a staple, coated in oatmeal – an indication of Scotland's culinary influence.

The major fishing ports of Ardglass and Portavogie bring in large quantities of traditional white fish such as cod and whiting as well as herring, mackerel and a wide range of shellfish. Prawns, in particular, are abundant.

Of course, the best way to appreciate fresh fish is to find a place to eat it. On Portrush Harbour, Co. Antrim, stands RAMORE RESTAURANT (Telephone: 0265 824313), where inventive, simple fish and shellfish dishes predominate.

MUSSELS AND SWEETBREADS IN A SPINACH PARCEL

1 lb/450 g lambs sweetbreads
5 lb/2.2 kg/10 cups mussels
3½ fl oz/100 ml/½ cup white wine
4 large spinach leaves
½ oz/14 g/1 tbs parsley, chopped

¼ lb/110 g mushrooms, finely chopped
1 medium onion, finely chopped
1 small onion, finely chopped
1 clove garlic, finely chopped
5 fl oz/125 ml/½ cup cream
1 oz/28 g/1 tbs chopped lemon balm

Prepare sweetbreads by boiling in water and simmering for 1 minute. Cool and discard gristle. Scrub the mussels and cook in a sealed pot with white wine, small onion and parsley until open. Cool and shell. Steam the spinach for 2 minutes and set aside. Cook finely chopped mushrooms, onion, garlic, cream and lemon balm in an open pan until the mixture is reduced and has thickened. Cool.

Combine mussels, sweetbreads and the reduction in equal quantities. Wrap in spinach and enclose in buttered foil. Steam for 6 minutes. Peel off foil. Serve with a puree of carrots, soft cheese or just with lemon quarters.

Serves 4

(CONNIE O'MAHONEY)

One of the great success stories of recent years is the SHELLFISH farming industry, with oysters in particular finding huge success locally and throughout the UK. Strangford and Carlingford Loughs are prime oyster growing areas and Northern Ireland as a whole produces around 178.8 tonnes of Pacific oysters per year.

IRISH OYSTER LOAVES

2 small bread rolls
2 oz/56 g/¼ cup melted butter
8 medium oysters
2 fl oz/60 ml/4 tbs soured cream
cayenne pepper or dash of Tabasco
salt and black pepper

Heat the oven to 220°C/425°F/Gas Mark 7. Carefully cut a topknot out of the rolls and scoop out the interior, leaving a hollow crust. Brush the crusts inside and out with half of the melted butter. Place in the oven for 10 minutes until crisp and golden. Meanwhile, scrub and open the oysters, keeping the liquor for the sauce. Cook the oysters in the remaining butter for a scant 60 seconds and then remove them and set aside. Add the oyster liquor to the pan juices together with the cream and seasonings. Heat gently, check seasoning, replace oysters and warm through but do not boil. Spoon the mixture into the rolls and replace the topknots. Serve immediately.

Serves 2

CUAN SEA FISHERIES LTD., Sketrick Island, Killinchy,
Newtownards, Co. Down.
Telephone: 0238 541461
Cuan is one of the province's most successful Pacific oyster
growers. The business has expanded to include a range of
prepared oyster dishes and a 24-hour mail order service.

At the same address is THE CUAN SEAFOOD SHOP, selling a wide
range of fresh and frozen seafood from all over the province and
sometimes beyond. The shop is open Monday to Friday, from
9.30 am to 5.00 pm.

If you would like to visit the beds where Cuan's oysters are
grown, call Dr. Jasper Parsons on 0238 541461 and he will be
happy to arrange a tour.

The numerous lakes, rivers and tributaries are famed for their
wonderful SALMON and TROUT. Keen anglers make special trips to
favourite stretches every year, knowing that the fish they catch
will be pure and flavoursome.

Lough Neagh, bordered by Tyrone, Antrim and Down is
particularly well known for its brown and silver eels. Smoked
eel is a Lough Neagh speciality, enjoyed as much today as it was
centuries ago and is still widely available.

SMOKED EEL SUPPLIERS

ERRINGTON TROUT FARM, Ballinamallard, Co. Fermanagh
Telephone: 036581 535

O'ROURKE SEAFOODS, Derryvale Industrial Estate, Newmills,
Dungannon, Co. Tyrone
Telephone: 086 87 48132

Farmers breed a mixture of beef and dairy cattle, both being
equally valuable. The dairy cattle are able to graze well on the
pasturelands while the sturdy beef cattle make use of the less
fertile ground.

Many traditional beef dishes have expanded their popularity
way beyond their origins – spiced beef, at one time reserved for
Christmas, is now recognised all over the world.

Far right: *Cattle grazing the lush pastures in Co Down*

IRISH SPICED BEEF

Begin preparations one week in advance.
1 ½ lb/675 g joint of brisket, boned and rolled

SPICE MIX

¼ oz/8 g/2 tsp ground bay leaves
4 g/1 tsp ground cloves
¼ oz/8 g/2 tsp ground mace
4 g/1 tsp ground black pepper
2 cloves garlic, crushed in salt
2 g/½ tsp allspice
4 g/1 tsp brown sugar
2 pts/1.1 litres/4 cups water
¼ lb/110 g/½ cup spiced pickling mixture or
4 g/1 tsp saltpetre and 8 oz/225 g/1 cup coarse salt
bouquet garni

2 carrots, sliced
2 onions, sliced
10 fl oz/290 ml/1 cup stout or Guinness
1 g/½ tsp ground cloves
2 g/½ tsp allspice

Combine all the spice mix ingredients together and place
them with the joint in an earthenware or glass container. Turn
daily and leave for one week. After this time wash the meat to
remove excess salt.

To cook the meat, place the joint on a bed of the sliced
carrot and onions. Pour over enough water to cover. Add the
spices and simmer for 4½–5 hours until tender. During the last
hour add the stout or Guinness. This dish may be served hot
or cold. If served cold, allow the meat to cool in the liquid,
then when cold, press together between two heavy plates.

Spiced beef is excellent cold with salads and a sour cream
dressing. Sometimes silverside or topside of beef is used. If
this is the case the method is the same but the cooking time is
reduced to 2–2½ hours.

Serves 6–8

(GRANGE LODGE DUNGANNON)

As in all regions where the land is not consistently fertile, sheep
farming is very important. Mutton was once a staple, used in
broths and stews, and is still much more accessible in Northern
Ireland than in other parts of Britain.

IRISH STEW, probably the most famous local dish, was eaten in
hard times, making use of old mutton, the inevitable potatoes
and any vegetables available. It was adopted by the English for
their hunt luncheons during the 19th century, when ham and
beef began to substitute the mutton.

Lamb from the province is enjoying something of a revival, its purity and flavour being recognised both locally and abroad. Northern Irish lamb has a high proportion of lean to fat and stringent quality controls ensure a superior product, quite able to compete with Welsh and English lamb.

The tradition of keeping a single pig in a sty at the bottom of the garden is strong here. The pigs would be fattened for the winter on mashed potato and turnips and as elsewhere in rural Britain, every part of the animal would eventually be utilised.

Many butchers' shops set up one-man businesses on the strength of local pigs, selling bacon, hams, trotters and chops. Bacon plays a particularly important role in the Northern Irish diet, its saltiness adding flavour to vegetable stews. It was also boiled with cabbage or pickled to be stored for the cold winter months.

Individual towns gained fame for their particular methods of curing hams. Belfast, Cookstown and Limerick all have hams named after them. Even today, the Belfast ham is sought after not only by the Irish but also by the English and Europeans.

Traditional dry-cured Belfast ham is available from:

WILLIAM PINKERTON & SON LTD., 21–25a Scotch Street, Armagh
Telephone: 0861 522434
William Pinkerton is a wholesale bacon factory, producing a range of cured and smoked meats. Belfast ham is cured on the premises and sold through local butchers. Wholesale buyers can visit Pinkerton's from 8.00 am to 4.30 pm Monday to Thursday and 8.00 am to 3.00 pm on Friday.

Pickled pigs' trotters, known as crubeens, were once eaten out of necessity but are now more associated with celebrations and a good crack. Pubs serve them on a Friday night and a party is not complete without a plate of crubeens for revellers to dig into.

Other traditional pork dishes include drisheen, a form of blood pudding, and tripe, which is usually served with potatoes and carrots, possibly with a white milky sauce.

It is not surprising that dairying is so important to Northern Ireland. The greenest pastures in the world give dairy cattle rich and creamy milk, so prolifically that diversification has become a significant part of the province's dairy industry. Approximately 1300M litres of milk are produced per year in Northern Ireland.

Irish butter accounts for over half the dairy production while cheese accounts for around 20%. There has been a recent upsurge of interest in the production of farmhouse cheese in many parts of Northern Ireland, with farmers taking unpasteurised milk from pure breed herds to make some of Britain's best-loved varieties.

WOODFORD DAIRY, 24 Finaghy Road South, Belfast
Telephone: 0232 614539
The Woodford Dairy specialises in goat's milk products, including its highly successful pasteurised goat's cheese, Rathdore. The Dairy sells on a wholesale basis only to supermarkets and food shops across the province, but visitors are very welcome to telephone to arrange a tour.

Distilling of grain, spring water and yeast has been going on in Ireland since at least the 6th century, when the idea was introduced into the country by missionary monks.

IRISH WHISKEY soon became popular further afield, praised by Henry II and Elizabeth I alike.

The difference between Irish and Scotch whiskey extends further than the additional 'e'. Irish whiskey is not flavoured by peat-smoking and is triple distilled, a costly and lengthy process. Scotch whisky is usually distilled twice, making it, some would say, less mellow than Irish.

OLD BUSHMILLS DISTILLERY, Bushmills, Co. Antrim
Telephone: 02657 31521
The oldest whiskey distillery in the land, Bushmills was first granted its licence to distil in 1608, but it is rumoured that illicit distilling went on at Bushmills long before this. Whatever the case, Bushmills whiskey is renowned throughout the world for its purity and distinctive flavour. It is a blended whiskey made of one single malt and one single grain with waters from the Rill adding a faint peaty flavour.

Tours are available around the distillery from Monday to Thursday 9.00 am to 12 noon and 1.30 pm to 3.30 pm and on Friday from 9.00 am to 11.00 am. Following the tour, you can buy souvenir bottles of Bushmills from one of the two distillery shops.

You can also stay at the BUSHMILLS INN, Main Street, Bushmills, Co. Antrim (Telephone: 02657 32339), and enjoy a glass of the province's most famous drink in the old-fashioned bar.

CHICKEN IN BUSHMILLS CREAM

4 chicken fillets
1 oz/28 g/1 tbs butter
1 fl oz/28 ml/2 tbs olive oil
salt and freshly ground black pepper
½ pt/190 ml/1 cup chicken stock
2 fl oz/56 ml/4 tbs Bushmills whiskey
¼ pt/1 50 ml/½ cup double cream
cashew nuts, to garnish
halved green grapes, to garnish

Heat the butter and oil in a heavy based frying pan. Season the fillets to taste and brown lightly on both sides. Remove from the pan and place in a flame proof casserole. Add the whiskey to the pan and flame. Add the stock and bring to the boil. Pour over the chicken and simmer gently for 25 minutes. Add the cream, stir well and simmer for a further 10 minutes until the sauce thickens or alternatively thicken with a little cornflour blended with milk. Serve sprinkled with cashew nuts and halved green grapes. Broccoli and champ are delicious with this dish.

Serves 4

(GRANGE LODGE DUNGANNON)

Top: *A hearty cooked Farmhouse breakfast*
Left: *The picturesque thatched Crosskey's Inn near Toome Bridge in Co Antrim dates back to the 19th Century*

WALES

THERE are few places as unspoilt as Wales. The North is mountainous and its rugged hillsides conceal hard slate, making it difficult to farm anything other than sheep and oats. The villages are more remote and unchanged, with a higher proportion of Welsh-speaking inhabitants than in any other part of Wales.

The Menai Straits, separating the Island of Angelsey from the mainland, now form the site for some of Britain's leading shellfish growers, with lobsters, scallops and oysters being amongst the first species to be successfully seeded. Fishing is still very important around the north Wales coast, where the cold Atlantic waters are warmed by the Gulf Stream.

Mid-Wales, where rolling hills full of Welsh sheep contrast with the thriving fishing towns on the coast, is the perfect appetiser for both south and north Wales.

South Wales has the ideal climatic and geographical characteristics for growing soft fruits. Consequently, there are many Pick-Your-Own ventures in Pembrokeshire and around the Gower coast, growing strawberries, blackberries, gooseberries and currants, while late summer sees the hedgerows and heathlands full of whinberries, the favourite Welsh berry. Known as bilberries elsewhere, whinberries look similar to blueberries but are smaller in size and they are a common feature in many Welsh puddings and bakery products.

Hospitality is never in short supply in Wales. From the remotest Powys farmhouse to the bustling small hotel, a welcome is always assured and generous portions of Welsh food are the order of the day. The big appetite of the farm-worker, the miner and the fisherman from days gone by has never really been forgotten.

A Welsh Hill Farm nestling in the rolling countryside on the Clwyd/Powys border

Welsh lamb grazing on the rich pastures which give it so much of its flavour

Places to stay in Wales include the incredibly grand, as well as the more homely. Of the former type, DOLMELYNLLYN HALL, in Dolgellau, Gwynedd (Telephone: 034 140 273) is a masterpiece, rambling over the Mawddach Valley. Dating back as far as the 16th century in parts, the Hall specialises in traditional cooking adapted to more imaginative palates, such as venison sausages with orange sauce or laverbread roulade with smoked salmon.

The justifiable reputation for the superior quality of Welsh mutton and lamb is largely due to the environment in which these sheep live and eat. They mature relatively slowly and are best consumed at the end of the summer, when they have had a chance to graze on the richer summer pastures and the abundance of herbs and flowers which grow in the Welsh fields give the meat a rich, distinctive flavour.

VARIATION OF WELSH LAMB SERVED WITH BRAISED LENTILS, SHERRY, VINEGAR AND WALNUT OIL

1 loin of lamb
2 fillets of lamb
4 oz/110 g lambs liver
3 whole lambs kidneys

LENTIL SALAD

4 oz/110 g/½ cup brown lentils
½ carrot
½ leek
½ celeriac
½ clove garlic
¼ oz/3 g/2 tsp tomato puree
4 g/1 tsp sugar
salt and freshly ground pepper
1 sprig of thyme
½ a bayleaf
½ pt/290 ml/1 cup chicken stock
1 oz/28 g/1 tbs butter

RICE CRACKERS

2 oz/56 g/¼ cup rice
8 oz/225 g/1½ cups plain flour
2 g/½ tsp salt

DRESSING AND SALAD

4 oz/110 g/½ cup mixed leaf salad (radichio, lollo rosso, frisee, etc.)
2 tomatoes
2 oz/56 g/¼ cup fine green beans
¼ pt/150 ml/½ cup walnut oil
½ fl oz/15 ml/1 tbs sherry vinegar
salt, pepper
1 sprig of chervil

Skin, then bone the loin of lamb, trim any nerve and sinews from the eye of the meat. Take out the fat which was originally attached and wrap around the loin. Tie, using butcher's string, at intervals about eight times to ensure the fat doesn't shrink during frying. Trim the lamb fillets, slice the liver and cut the kidneys in half lengthways, removing the gristle from the middle.

Soak the lentils for 2–3 hours, then blanch in boiling, salt water, don't refresh. Peel and cut the vegetables into small cubes. In a saucepan add an eye of butter and slowly cook for 2–3 minutes before adding the garlic, tomato puree and sugar. Add the lentils, the herbs and the chicken stock and cook for approximately 5–10 minutes, until tender. Set to one side.

Cook the rice, drain and blend in a blender. Add the flour and blend to form a dough. The rice may also be kneaded with the flour by hand if the blender is not available. The dough should not be sticky. Roll out thinly and cut into fine strips about 2 in/5 cm in length. Deep fry in hot oil and drain in a cloth, sprinkle with salt.

Prepare and wash the salad leaves, dry well. Blanch the tomatoes, skin and cut into squares removing the seeds. Pick over the beans, cut in half and cook refreshing in cold water. Whisk the vinegar and oil together and season.

Season and pan fry the loin on the stove in a little oil for about 5–10 minutes. Then fry the fillet, season and fry the floured liver and kidneys. Mix the lentils with a little dressing and serve on a plate. Season the leaf salad, tomato and fine beans, add a spoonful of dressing and arrange on the plates. Place the lamb on the plates with the salad and top with the rice crackers and chervil.

Serves 4–6

(MARK SALTER AT LLANGOED HALL)

WILLIAM JONES & SONS, 1–3 High Street, Newtown, Powys.
Telephone: 0686 625509
Deep in the very heart of mid-Wales, surrounded on all sides by brooding grey hills, the market town of Newtown serves the numerous small villages which nestle in the folds of the hills. William Jones & Sons is a family run butcher's shop established in 1880, now being run by the 4th generation of Jones's. Welsh lamb is bought from a farmer in nearby Llanidloes in whole carcasses, then expertly cut by the Jones family. As well as prime cuts, they also do a bustling trade in lamb sausages and pies, all made on the premises.

CAWL is another staple which featured often in the Welsh diet. It has many permutations, varying in its exact ingredients and cooking method in each village or district. However, its basic ingredients are lamb or most often bacon, leeks and cabbage –

an indication of its humble origins. The bacon is cooked in a large pot hanging over the open fire, together with the vegetables, possibly with oatmeal to thicken it.

Pork became a mainstay in Wales, being both economical and versatile. All parts of the pig were used, resulting in enduringly popular dishes such as faggots and blood pudding. Bacon has always formed a significant part of the Welsh diet, too, eaten fried or grilled for breakfast or put in the cooking pot to keep fish and meat moist.

ROBERTS OF PORT DINORWIC, Griffiths Crossing, Caernarfon, Gwynedd
Telephone: 0286 76111
Old mixes happily with new at Roberts, overlooking the Menai Straits in North Wales. The company was founded in 1924, when a small oven was installed at the back of the village's pork butcher's shop. Roberts pork pies soon became the talk of the town and are still made to the same high standards but on a much more modern level. In bringing their operation up to present EC standards, Roberts have taken great care not to lose any of their authenticity. The range of products includes pies, sausages, hams and cooked meats, all of which are made to the same traditional recipes as they were back in 1924.

WARM SALAD OF MONKFISH, CARMARTHEN HAM AND
MUSHROOMS

1½ lb/675 g monkfish tail
4–6 oz/110–170 g/1 cup sliced Carmarthen ham
2 oz/56 g/½ cup button mushrooms
olive oil
½ onion, chopped
1 clove of garlic, chopped
vinaigrette
salad leaves
pepper

Remove the monkfish from the bone and trim off the skin. Cut into 1 in/2½ cm cubes. Cut ham into thin strips. Break the mushrooms into large pieces. Heat a little olive oil in a 10 in/25 cm non-aluminium pan. Toss in the fish, onion, garlic, mushrooms and ham. Saute until the fish is firm, 1–2 minutes. Remove from the heat and add 100 ml/3½ fl oz vinaigrette. Arrange the salad leaves on 6 plates. Divide the ingredients between the plates and trickle the warm vinaigrette in the pan over everything. Season with pepper and serve.

Serves 6

(CHRIS CHOWN AT PLAS BODEGROES RESTAURANT)

Until coal mining and quarrying were introduced, Wales was predominantly rural, made up of smallholdings and tenanted farms, growing oats and wheat.

During the 16th century, the countryside was dotted with watermills, driven by the fast rivers, milling local oats and, later, wheat and barley. As a result, bakery products have become very important to Wales, as they not only make use of abundant local ingredients but also provide satisfying and economical meals for its hard-working countrymen and women.

The open hearth of the traditional Welsh cottage was the centre of the family home. As well as providing the heat for the vast pot which hung above it, its embers heated the flat iron disk known as a bakestone. The bakestone was common in all countries with strong Celtic backgrounds and was used for cooking pancakes, breads, scones and oatcakes.

The bakestone has left its mark on the country's culinary heritage. Cakes are still regularly baked on a griddle in markets across the land to satisfy the demand for traditional Welsh bakery. Swansea market, for example, is teeming with people eager to buy freshly griddled Welsh cakes seven days of the week.

NANCY MORGAN, 84 Bryn-y-Mor Road, Swansea
Telephone: 0792 460981
Locals and visitors alike flock to Nancy Morgan's shop in Swansea, with its beautifully maintained frontage proclaiming the sale of WELSH CAKES. The shop actually sells a whole variety of traditional griddle-baked Welsh specialities, including bread, oatcakes, pancakes and bara brith. There is also a stall in Swansea market, where the cakes can be seen being baked every day of the week.

As in the North of England and Scotland, 'high tea' is an eagerly anticipated meal in Wales, made up of a huge range of satisfying bread and cakes, such as bara brith and teisen lap. Bara Brith means 'speckled bread' and was originally made from the last of the day's bread dough into which was thrown a handful of currants; teisen lap, on the other hand, was given to Welsh miners for lunch, as it held together well without being dry enough to make them thirsty.

The addition of fruit and spices is a particular feature of Welsh bakery. Spices were introduced to Wales by the Crusaders, who brought many back from the Holy Land. The same combination is found in many traditional Welsh puddings, too. Rice pudding, making use of plentiful milk supplies, is still an integral part of many Sunday lunches, while creamy puds such as junket and syllabub are enduringly popular across the whole of Wales.

The leek is the only vegetable indigenous to Wales and as such, it became the country's emblem in the 7th century, after St. David's troops used a leek to identify themselves in battle against the Saxons, and is sometimes still worn on St. David's Day in March. Surprisingly, perhaps, to modern tastes, the country's other symbol, the daffodil, was originally viewed as a food rather than a flower, eaten for pudding with figs!

WELSH SALT DUCK WITH ONION SAUCE

2, 4–5 lb/1.8–2.3 kg ducks

BRINE SOLUTION
10½ pts/6 litres/21 cups warm water
21 oz/600 g/2½ cups coarse sea salt
9 oz/225 g/1 cup sugar
1 oz/28 g/1 tbs saltpetre

ONION SAUCE
2 oz/56 g/¼ cup butter
1 lb/450 g/3 cups onions, peeled and thinly sliced
1 pt/570 g/2 cups milk or stock
pinch of ground mace
pinch of ground nutmeg
salt
freshly ground black pepper
1 oz/28 g/1 tbs plain flour

Soak the two ducks in the brine solution for 2–3 days. After soaking, wash the ducks and simmer *very* gently in fresh water with a handful of salt in a double boiler until tender. Check after one hour.

Meanwhile, make the onion sauce. Melt 1 oz/28 g/1 tbs butter in a large pan and slowly cook the sliced onions, stirring from time to time, until they are soft but not brown. Meanwhile, heat the milk or stock in another pan. Add the milk or stock to the onions, season with the mace and nutmeg and add salt and pepper to taste. Simmer for 10–15 minutes, then strain, reserve liquid and onions. Melt the remaining 1 oz/28 g/1 tbs of butter. Add the flour, stirring with a spoon and cook gently for 2–3 minutes. Remove from the heat and gradually add the onion liquid, stirring all the time to avoid lumps. Chop all the drained onions very finely, or rub them through a sieve and add them to the sauce, stirring well. Heat through again. Take off all skin and fat and carefully carve the breast in thick slices and arrange with the leg left on the bone on a bed of onion sauce, one breast and leg per person.

Serves 4
(POMEGRANATES RESTAURANT)

A patchwork of green fields near Dwygyfylchi

Root vegetables grow well in Welsh soil; potatoes and turnips are widely grown, often served mashed together in equal quantities, a dish known as punchnep.

The area around Pembroke is particularly noted for its excellent early potatoes, with Welsh growers racing those in Kent and the West Country to get the first potatoes of the season to market. This can be as early as May, although they are usually not widely available until mid August.

Most of Wales's dairy industry is based in the South, where the cattle can graze on lusher, greener pastures. The climate is also warmer and wetter, two essential characteristics of a good dairying area.

Milk which does not go for bottling enables many farmers to engage in financially rewarding diversification operations. Welsh butter has a salty taste, a throwback to the days when so much butter was produced that salt was added as a preservation aid. Wales also enjoys a strong ice-cream making tradition; Italian immigrants, especially in the South, lend their names and talents to many Welsh ice cream manufacturing companies.

As well as butter and ice cream, milk supplies go to make the world famous Welsh cheeses, including Caerphilly as well as several newly developed farmhouse cheeses.

VARIETIES OF 'EARLIES' GROWN IN WALES

HOME GUARD: floury white flesh. Best boiled and served with plenty of salty Welsh butter.

ARRAN COMET: very creamy, firm flesh. May be boiled, chipped or used in salads.

ULSTER SCEPTRE: firm, waxy flesh. Again, good for boiling, chipping or in salads.

DUTCH PREMIER: a relative newcomer, increasing in popularity. Its pale yellow flesh is particularly suitable for chips.

PATRICK'S WELSH RAREBIT

2 eggs
3 oz/225 g/1 cup grated hard cheese (eg. Cheddar)
2 oz/56 g/¼ cup melted butter
2 cloves garlic
1 oz/28 g/1 tbs Welsh grain mustard
15 ml/1 tbs Worcestershire sauce
4 g/1 tsp salt
4 g/1 tsp grated horseradish

Blend all the ingredients to a smooth paste and spread on brown toast. Grill until brown.

(POMEGRANATES RESTAURANT)

CAERPHILLY

Originally made in and around Caerphilly in Glamorgan, authentic Caerphilly is much rarer today, although attempts are being made to revive it. It was widely produced in South Wales from around 1800 to 1941, where it was popular with miners, but went the way of so many farmhouse cheeses with the advent of war.

Modern Caerphilly is said to be harder and whiter than the original cheese, with a stronger taste of salt. It has a close, flaky texture and a mild flavour.

CAERPHILLY CHEESEMAKERS IN WALES

Please telephone first to make appointment to visit.
FELIN GERNOS DAIRY, Maesllyn, Llandysul, Dyfed
Telephone: 023 975 362

DAIRY CREST, Four Crosses Creamery, Llanymynech, Powys
Telephone: 0691 830212

LLANGLOFFAN

One of the newer Welsh cheeses, this full-fat hard cheese made with the unpasteurised milk of Jersey herds is becoming increasingly renowned all over Britain. It forms a natural crust and begins ripening after about 6 weeks, taking up to 12 months to fully mature. Available from LLANGLOFFAN FARM, Castle Morris, Near Mathry, Haverfordwest, Dyfed.

PENCARREG

Another newly successful Welsh cheese, whose smooth creamy texture develops with maturation. It is an organically produced soft cheese and originates from the Lampeter area. Available from WELSH ORGANIC FOODS LTD, Lampeter, Dyfed.

For one of the best arrays of Welsh farmhouse cheeses, CARMARTHEN COVERED MARKET in Dyfed is the place to go. Every Wednesday, around a dozen Welsh cheesemakers gather to display and sell their cheeses. The choice will include Caerphilly, Llangloffan and many less well-known varieties and cheeses may be bought whole or in pieces. It is a wonderful way to discover which is your favourite.

Swansea market also has an excellent cheese stall called CURDS & WHEY, selling a wide range of Welsh farmhouse cheese, including ewe's and goat's milk varieties. Swansea market is open Monday to Saturday from 9.00 am to 5.00 pm.

Llangloffan

Caerphilly

WELSH CHEESEMAKERS
Please telephone first to make appointment to visit.

MESEN FACH FARM, Bethania, Nr. Llanon, Dyfed.
Telephone: 097 423348
• Acorn – ewe's milk, hard, full-fat, unpasteurised.

RACHEL'S DAIRY, Brynllys, Borth, Dyfed
Telephone: 0970 871489
• Pencarreg – unpasteurised milk from mixed herd, full-fat, soft, sold young

LLANBOIDY FARMHOUSE, Cilowen Uchaf, Login, Whitland, Dyfed
Telephone: 099 46 448303
• Llanboidy – full-fat, hard, unpasteurised Red Poll milk, matured for 2 months
• Welsh Farmhouse – as above, matured for 8–10 weeks

FFERM GLYNEITHRINIOG, Pontseli, Boncath, Dyfed – no visitors
• Cenarth Cearffli – unpasteurised vegetarian cheese
• Cenarth Farmhouse Cheese – as above but softer, also available matured

HADARI, Tyn Rhyd, Maerdy, Corwen, Clwyd – no visitors
• Hadari – goat's milk, hard, low or full fat, also available for vegetarians

---

CRISP PASTRY PARCEL OF WELSH FARMHOUSE CHEESES

*8 oz/225 g hard cheese (eg, Llanboidy, Cardigan, Ty'n Grug,
Caron)*
½ Bramley apple
few sultanas
few walnut halves
1 oz/28 g/1 tbs mustard
1 oz/28 g/1 tbs chopped chives
2 eggs
pepper
8–10 oz/225–285 g filo, strudel or spring roll pastry
2 oz/56 g melted butter

Heat the oven to 220°C/400°F/Gas Mark 6. Grate the cheese,
chop the apple and mix together with all the other
ingredients. Chill to firm up. Place in the centre of filo pastry
sheets folded in two. Wrap into rolls or small squares in
pastry. Brush with melted butter, place on a greased baking
tray and bake in oven for 10 minutes, until golden brown.
Serve with a dressed salad.

(CHRIS CHOWN AT PLAS BODEGROES RESTAURANT)

Wales reaps the benefit of around 750 miles of coastline, from
the wide inward sweep of Cardigan Bay, to the harbour-lined
Bristol Channel and the rocky and tempestuous Irish Sea.

Sea fishing has survived as an important part of the Welsh
food industry, with many locally caught species such as bass
and grey mullet being sold locally, too, rather than transported
away to the English markets. Skate is also plentiful, as are Dover
sole and plaice. But the most popular Welsh fish must surely be
the 'sewin', or sea trout, a member of the brown trout family.
The Rivers Teifi, Towy and Claddua teem with sewin and fishmongers' slabs all over the country are kept well stocked from
March until the end of August.

VIN SULLIVAN OF ABERGAVENNY, 4 Frogmore Street,
Abergavenny, Gwent
Telephone: 0873 6989
Probably Wales's most famous specialist food shop, Vin Sullivan
supplies many of the country's top hotels and catering establishments with the finest local produce, from 100 different types of
fish and shellfish to a wide range of poultry and game products.
This does not mean that the individual consumer is forgotten;
customers may pop in for laverbread or cockles or Welsh honey
at any time and receive the same friendly efficient service.

*There is no shortage of shellfish in Wales, with some of Britain's finest
crab caught off Pembrokeshire's rocky coastline*

MARINATED HERRINGS WITH BASIL,
DILL, ROCK SALT & SESAME

1 very fresh herring, filleted and skinned
1 oz/28 g/2 tbs freshly chopped basil
1 oz/28 g/2 tbs freshly chopped dill
2 oz/56 g/¼ cup toasted sesame seeds
rock salt
freshly ground black pepper
lemon juice
white wine
sesame oil

Slice the herring as you would smoked salmon, as thin as
possible and place on a plastic tray or a deep plate. Sprinkle
liberally with the herbs, sesame seeds, rock salt and pepper.
Mix equal quantities of lemon juice, white wine and sesame
oil together and whisk. Pour just enough of the liquid over
the fish to cover it. Place in a refrigerator for 12–14 hours.
This dish is delicious eaten with melba toast and fresh
summer salad.

Serves 4

(ANDY TAYLOR AT MAES-Y-NEUADD HOTEL)

Since at least Roman times, COCKLES have been collected by
hand from the beaches around the Gower Peninsula every day
of the week except Sunday. The women and young men of the
Gower villages wait until the tide is out and then trek for around
4 miles across the seaweed strewn rocks and muddy estuaries
into Carmarthen Bay.

Small cockles are gathered from the wet sands and mud flats
and thrown into sacks. The full sacks are then loaded onto
horse-drawn carts which stagger back to the mainland to the
boiling sheds for washing and shelling.

No vehicles are allowed on the cockle beds and it is unlikely
that any form of mechanisation will ever make this ancient task
any easier. The only change to take place in recent years is the
replacement of donkeys by horses to draw the carts.

The cockles are generally sold in local markets or door-to-
door and are eaten plain with just a sprinkling of vinegar and
pepper.

LAVER

Wales is one of the few areas in Britain which can truly boast
that it continues to make the most of its abundant local ingredients; the fact that LAVER, or seaweed, is still a very important
part of the Welsh diet is proof in itself.

Laver is collected from the rocks around the Pembroke and
Gower coasts, as it has been for centuries. It is taken to the
numerous small factories which line the coast to be boiled for
around 5 hours. The laver is then made into bread by mixing
with oatmeal. Laverbread is sold in coastal markets and fishmongers' shops and is generally eaten for breakfast, perhaps
with a sprinkling of oatmeal and black pepper and almost defin-
itely with bacon. Most coastal markets have stalls which sell
fresh laverbread but it is also available in tins.

*Cockle picking on the Gower
Peninsula, which is still only
done by hand*

CILOWEN UCHAF, Login, Whitland, Dyfed
Telephone: 09946 448303
This dairy farm produces predominantly cheeses from its organically-managed herd of Red Poll cattle. Red Polls, incidentally, are becoming increasingly rare in Britain and are worth seeing for that reason alone. The farm shop also sells laverbread and other local produce.

When the Romans came to Wales, they imported many European and English HERBS to complement the wonderful fish and shellfish they found there. They planted a wide variety of herbs which still grow wild over much of uncultivated Wales, including fennel, coriander, sorrel, dill, tansy and thyme.

Most health food and wholefood shops, of which there are a great number in inland Wales, sell a wide range of fresh local herbs and herbalism is still taken very seriously.

WELSHPOOL HERBS & SPICES, 24 High Street, Welshpool, Powys
Telephone: 0938 3180
Open Monday to Saturday 9.00 am to 5.00 pm, closed Thursday. An enormous range of fresh herbs from local gardens, as well as dried herbs on request. All produce sold in the shop is organically-produced, including mustards, jams and honey.

ROSEMARY BLANQUETTE OF LAMB WITH ROSEMARY DUMPLINGS

1 lb/450 g lean lamb, diced
1 pt/570 ml/2 cups double cream
4 oz/110 g/½ cup rosemary

DUMPLINGS

2 oz/110 g/¼ cup butter
2 oz/110 g/¼ cup flour
1 egg
salt and pepper
chopped rosemary leaves

Heat the oven to 190°C/375°F/Gas Mark 5. Drop the lamb in boiling water for 40–45 seconds, rinse off in cold water. This will help to keep the diced lamb in one piece when cooked. Place the lamb pieces in an oven proof dish and cover with fresh water. Pick off the leaves of rosemary and keep for the dumplings. Place the stalks in with the lamb, cover and cook in the oven for 2–3 hours depending on the size of the pieces of meat. When cooked, remove the lamb pieces and keep warm. Discard the rosemary stalks and boil the liquid to

reduce by half, then add the double cream and reduce slightly to thicken.

To make the dumplings. Cream the butter and then mix in the flour. Gradually beat in the egg, then mix in the rosemary leaves and season slightly. Pull off little pieces of dough and gently poach in boiling salted water for 2–3 minutes. Serve hot with the lamb, with a piece of home made crusty bread to dip in the sauce.

Serves 4
(ANDY TAYLOR AT MAES-Y-NEUADD HOTEL)

Pure Welsh Spring water

The abundance of wild flowers and berries has enabled the rural Welsh to produce delicious country wines and cordials, although most production takes place on a domestic level.

Mead, made with fermented Welsh honey, was also once widely produced, although it is somewhat rarer today.

As far as Welsh viticulture is concerned, the industry is still very much in its infancy. This is despite the fact that the Romans planted vines on the south-facing slopes of Gwent and Dyfed, to make wines to accompany the wealth of natural produce.

The pure mountain springs of Wales have given Britain some of its finest and most successful mineral waters, such as Ty-Nant, in its award-winning bluer-than-blue bottle.

WELSH SPRING WATERS

BRECON BEACONS NATURAL WATER
Telephone: 0269 850115
Carbonated and still – available all over the UK

PRYSG NATURAL MINERAL WATER
Telephone 055 935 627
Carbonated and still – available all over the UK

GLYNDWR
Telephone: 0970 86229
Carbonated and still – available in Dyfed only

TY-NANT
Telephone: 0570 423037

NORTHERN ENGLAND

THE north of England is more or less divided into two halves by the long range of the PENNINES. Stretching down from the Scottish border as far as Derbyshire in the Midlands, the Pennines continue to act as a barrier between east and west. The vast open moorlands and heaths of the Northern reaches of YORKSHIRE and NORTHUMBERLAND are rich in both feathered and furred game. August 12th, known as 'The Glorious 12th', heralds the shooting season for grouse, shortly followed by pheasant, partridge, hare, wild duck and, in more wooded areas, deer. Game is particularly important in the mountainous regions, as it contributes towards many of the dishes hearty enough to satisfy the appetites of hikers and fell-runners.

The glorious autumn shades of Wasdale in Cumbria

JUGGED HARE

1 hare – cut into pieces, reserve the blood from the hare
4 oz/110 g/½ cup butter
1 onion, sliced
2 carrots, sliced
1 stick celery, sliced
2 cloves garlic
1 sprig of fresh rosemary
2 bay leaves
7 fl oz/200 ml/1 cup robust red wine
2 pts/1.1 litres/4 cups chicken stock
salt and pepper

TO GARNISH

8 oz/225 g/1 ¾ cup button onions
8 oz/225 g/2 cups smoked bacon, cut into strips
good handful of cubed bread
parsley, chopped

Preheat the oven to 180°C/350°F/Gas Mark 4. Brown the

Allotment gardening provides many homes with fresh vegetables and salads

pieces of hare in half of the butter and place in a casserole dish. Fry all the vegetables and herbs in the remaining half of the butter. When the vegetables are lightly browned pour in half the red wine and then place all the ingredients into the casserole with the chicken stock. Cook in the oven for approximately 2 hours, occasionally topping up with water if necessary. Boil the button onions and the bacon, separately, until cooked. Drain and allow to cool. Fry the onions, bacon and cubed bread until golden brown. Keep warm. Remove hare from casserole dish and keep warm. Pour the stock from the dish through a sieve into a pan, skim off any grease and season with salt and pepper. Thicken the stock over the heat by adding the remaining red wine and blood from the hare, stir continuously, but do not boil. Once this has thickened, place the hare onto a serving dish and pour the sauce over. Sprinkle with parsley and garnish with bacon, onions and bread croutons.

Serves 4
(PAUL HEATHCOTE AT HEATHCOTES)

FORCEMEAT BALLS

These can be added to the jugged hare
4 oz/110 g/ cup ham
8 oz/225 g cold cooked chicken
1 small onion
4 g/1 tsp lemon peel
4 g/1 tsp orange peel
8 oz/225 g/1 cup breadcrumbs
4 g/1 tsp chopped parsley
salt and pepper
1 egg
a little milk, for binding
1 pan of simmering chicken stock

Mince the ham and cold cooked chicken in a food processor. Add all the other ingredients to the meat, the egg being added last. Add a little milk if necessary to bind the ingredients together. Shape into small dumplings. Place the dumplings in a pan of simmering chicken stock for 15 minutes.

Serves 4

(PAUL HEATHCOTE AT HEATHCOTES)

Although much of the North-West of England is now industrialised, agriculture is still very important to the region, as the number of market gardens and farm shops shows. There is also a long-established enthusiasm for 'allotment gardening'. People who live in houses without or with gardens not long enough for growing vegetables can rent strips of land on which they can cultivate their own root and salad vegetables.

Large glasshouses also keep the cold off many of Britain's favourite salad vegetables, such as lettuce, tomatoes and cucumbers. Most of the produce grown in the region is sold locally, either at market or through wholesalers to supermarkets and other retail outlets.

North Yorkshire proudly produces around 70% of Britain's early, or 'forced', rhubarb. Gooseberries also thrive in the North, widely grown on a commercial scale in Lancashire and all over the region both in the wild and in allotments.

On the west coast, lies industrial Merseyside with its unofficial capital, Liverpool.

CROXTETH HALL AND COUNTRY PARK, Liverpool
Telephone 051 228 5311
Croxteth Hall is a working country estate incorporating a farm of rare breed animals, impressive walled fruit and herb gardens and greenhouses, all set in acres of beautiful parkland.

The west coast, bordering Lancashire, is dotted with perennially popular sea-side resorts, such as BLACKPOOL and MORECAMBE. Strolling along the promenade, eating fresh cockles with vinegar out of a paper cone, visitors should buy a stick of Blackpool rock – a long, pink and white stick of sugary confectionery with the letters BLACKPOOL running all the way through it. To find out how the letters get through the rock, visit the Coronation Rock Company where Blackpool rock has been made by hand since 1927.

CORONATION ROCK COMPANY, 11 Cherry Tree Road North, Blackpool
Telephone: 0253 62366
Open to visitors all year round
Monday to Thursday 9.00 am to 3.30 pm
Friday 9.00 am to 2.30 pm
Closed at the weekend

Fresh fish can be bought from the dockside merchants in many Northern seaports, but trading begins very early. Unlike the Southern markets, fish is also sold at market on Mondays. The choice is likely to be quite traditional – cod, haddock, coley, huss, skate, whiting, witch – but the quality will be excellent.

FISH AND CHIPS

Locally-caught fish was once much cheaper, before its true value was realised; fried fish, combined with that other economical staple, the potato, gave Britain its famous fish and chip shops. Standards do vary, but lightly battered fresh haddock, with a golden pile of chips and, for the true connoisseur, a side order of 'mushy' peas (marrowfat peas soaked overnight and then boiled) is a truly delicious treat.

Harry Ramsden's, Guisley, Bradford, Yorkshire, is probably the most famous fish and chip shop in Britain, attracting thousands of tourists annually. However, there are other smaller less well-known establishments which have gained great local respect, with loyal customers returning year after year.

STEELS CORNER HOUSE CAFE, Market Place, Cleethorpes, Humberside
Telephone: 0472 692644
With its gingham table cloths, perfectly-positioned cruets and invariably excellent food, Steels has been attracting coachloads of hungry customers for years. In fact, visitors to Cleethorpes tend to look forward to Steels' fish, chips and mushy peas much more than to the expanse of dark, wet sand along the sea front.

It is not all fish and chips up North, though. Morecambe in Lancashire lands small, brown shrimps so renowned for their distinctive flavour and texture that they are called Morecambe Bay Shrimps, highly-prized throughout the country. North Shields on the east coast has its own local fleet which goes out fishing for langoustines during the winter.

Two areas in the North are famed for their kippers, Craster in Northumberland and the Isle of Man, off the North-West coast. In Craster, local herrings are smoked over slow oak fires to a 100 year-old recipe. And Manx kippers (from the Isle of Man) are free from any artificial dyes, leaving them pale gold rather than dark brown or bright yellow. Both types of kipper have specific seasons, so are only available for limited periods, making their value shoot up even higher.

The LAKE DISTRICT is 30 miles across, containing lakes formed by the outward thrust of ice-age glaciers radiating from central rocks. A region of outstanding beauty and variety, the Lake District is a combination of mountains, hillside paths, low sheltered valleys and steep-sided ridges of loose slate. The mountains seem to dominate, casting shadows over the villages in the valleys.

Following the many country paths along wooded hillsides, Rydal Water and Grasmere slide into view and walkers are rewarded with the majestic sights which inspired the poet William Wordsworth. Around the shores of Lake Windermere grows the Witherslack damson, ripe for picking in the Autumn.

The vast county of NORTH YORKSHIRE spreads across from the stark east coast to the border with Lancashire, taking in a large portion of the Pennines. This is a wild and windswept place, so dramatic that Emily Bronte set *Wuthering Heights* near Haworth, one of the more desolate moorland villages.

SEAFOOD AND YORKSHIRE PUDDING

YORKSHIRE PUDDING MIX
2 eggs
3 oz/85 g/½ cup flour
½ pt/290 ml/1 cup milk
2 g/1 tsp melted butter
seasoning

SEAFOOD
8 scallops in the shell
8 langoustines
½ lb/225 g wild salmon
8 oysters

SAUCE
langoustine shells
½ lb/225 g/1 cup finely diced shallot, carrot and celery
4 g/1 tsp tomato paste

1 pt/570 ml/2 cups fish stock
white wine
brandy
¼ lb/110 g/½ cup unsalted butter, cubed

fresh herbs to garnish

Heat the oven to 200°C/400°F/Gas Mark 6. First prepare the Yorkshire pudding. Sift the flour and salt together, make a well in the centre and drop in the eggs with one third of the milk. Stir to a smooth paste, beating thoroughly and gradually adding the remaining milk. Set to one side.

Prepare all the seafood by cleaning the scallops, peeling the langoustines, opening the oysters and cutting 4 escalopes of salmon. Then start the sauce by sweating the langoustine shells with the diced shallot, carrot and celery. Stir in the tomato paste. Pour in the brandy and white wine and set alight, shaking the pan gently until the flames die away. Pour in the fish stock. Bring to the boil and then simmer for one hour.

Pour the Yorkshire pudding batter into 4 greased individual patty tins and cook for 15–20 minutes. Strain the sauce through a fine sieve, mix in the butter and check the seasoning. Pan fry the langoustines, scallops, salmon and poach the oysters very quickly. Place a Yorkshire pudding in

The majestic serenity of Rydal Water which provided such inspiration to the poet, William Wordsworth

the centre of each warm plate, arrange the seafood around and then add the sauce. Garnish with fresh herbs – tarragon, chervil or dill.

Serves 4
(THIERRY AUBUGEAU AT CHESHAM'S RESTAURANT, LONDON)

The fact that many dishes using OFFAL are still very popular all over the North is a tribute to the resourcefulness of its cooks in hard times. Waste was not allowed and every part of the animal was used in one dish or another. Not all types of offal are as widely available as they once were, although it is usually possible to persuade an enthusiastic butcher to seek them out.

Liver: Highly nutritious and widely available. Calf's liver is the most exclusive, while lamb's and pig's liver are excellent for the traditional British breakfast dish of liver and bacon.

Trotters: In Lancashire, pigs' trotters are cooked with onions and seasoning and served with parsley sauce. They need to be cooked for around 2½ hours in a white stock for the meat to be tender enough to strip easily away from the trotters. Sheep

trotter meat is also rolled in that great Northern staple, oatmeal, in Lancashire.

Brains: Now scarce enough to be viewed as luxurious, calf's brains are the most delicate. Lamb's brains are more common and can be stewed in creamy, thick sauces or sliced and fried in breadcrumbs.

Chitterlings: The small intestines, together with other entrails, of the pig. Chitterlings are becoming popular once again, as they are economical and tasty, and in Co. Durham, jellied chitterlings are eaten with onions.

Cow heel: Now extremely rare, cow heel was once served boiled with parsley sauce or in a vegetable stew in many Northern counties.

Tripe: Before fish and chip shops rose to become the No. 1 take-away outlet in Britain, the North (and many of the Midland counties) were populated by shops selling tripe and onions. Tripe comes from three of the four stomachs of the cow and is usually sold ready-boiled.

Many of the traditionally Northern dishes using offal or less expensive cuts of meat are now favourites all over Britain. For example, BLACK PUDDING made from pig's blood, oatmeal, barley and lots of seasoning, is eaten by thousands as part of the great British breakfast. FAGGOTS, too, are no longer the sole domain of Northerners – a mixture of liver, kidney, belly, heart and brain bound together with a pig's caul, they are served cold but can also be shallow-fried for breakfast.

There are specifically Northern blends of sausage, too, more often than not including oatmeal, barley and herbs. In Yorkshire, short fat sausages are made with beef rather than pork. Further north in Cumberland, there is the eponymous coiled sausage, containing only pork, herbs and spices and measuring up to 4′ long. Far from being a localised speciality, the Cumberland sausage is readily available throughout the country.

LARGE WHITE YORKSHIRE PIG

This hardy, widely-bred animal has long, strong legs to support its hefty body (ideally proportioned for hams) and clean, pink skin covered with small golden hairs. It is particularly popular in the North because each part can be made use of – the knuckles are excellent in stews and hot pots, the trotters are large enough for cooking and its ample flesh makes superb bacon.

The York Ham was once a common sight all over Britain. The traditional cure is equal portions of salt and sugar with an ounce of saltpetre, rubbed into the ham, which was then turned in brine. Rumour has it that the ham was once smoked over wood shavings left over from the building of York Minster. York Ham is now enjoying a revival, and is more widely available in its true form.

HARRIS – LEEMING BAR, Leases Road, Leeming Bar,
Northallerton, North Yorkshire
Telephone: 0677 22661
Please contact Steve Smith to arrange a visit.

The Harris Bacon Group was originally established in Wiltshire at
a pork butcher's shop curing and selling Irish bacon, taken from
pigs on their way to London. Generations of Harrises have run
the company, enjoying success as their high quality hams and
bacons and traditional production methods found great favour
outside, as well as inside, the region.

When the Irish Famine in the 19th century caused pig supplies
to become severely limited, Harris were forced to find an
alternative curing schedule – the English had always cured in the
winter and salted in the summer. A trip to America provided the
answer; curing could take place during the summer, too, in an
ice-cooled building. It worked in England and Harris patented the
idea almost immediately.

Amongst the range of Harris products is the York Ham,
produced in the Leeming Bar factory since 1978 to an old
Victorian recipe. A long maturation period gives the ham its
tender texture and distinctive mellow flavour.

A tasty traditional Lancashire Hot Pot

LANCASHIRE HOT POT

8–12 middle neck of lamb chops or best end of neck chops
8 oz/225 g/1½ cups onions, peeled and thinly sliced
4 carrots, peeled and sliced
salt and black pepper
2 g/½ tsp mixed herbs
1½ lbs/675 g potatoes, peeled and sliced
½ pt/290 ml/1¼ cups good stock
1 oz/28 g/1 tbs butter or margarine, melted
chopped parsley, to garnish

Heat oven to 170°C/325°F/Gas Mark 3. Remove any excess fat
from the chops and layer them in a large casserole with the
onions, carrots, seasonings and herbs. Cover with a thick layer
of overlapping slices of potato. Bring the stock up to the boil
and pour over the potatoes and then brush them liberally with
melted butter or margarine. Cover the casserole with a lid or foil
and cook in the oven for 2 hours. Remove the lid from the
casserole, increase the oven temperature to 220°C/425°F/Gas
Mark 7, and continue cooking for about 20 minutes or so, until
the potatoes are well browned. Sprinkle with chopped parsley
and serve.

Serves 4

MUTTON was once a staple throughout Britain and today it is only
in the more isolated regions, and in the North of England
particularly, that it has survived as a relatively important sheep
product. All over the hills and farmlands of the North, the
hardier breeds of sheep flourish. They have to be strong enough
to withstand howling winds and harsh winters and to survive
on what they can crop from the ground when bad weather
restricts deliveries of prepared feed.

Most sheep in the region are now farmed for lamb rather than
mutton. The spring lamb, usually available from June to August,
is particularly tender and succulent.

Despite the decline in popularity of mutton over recent years,
many mutton-based dishes have survived, even if the mutton
has been replaced by lamb or, in some cases, beef. Lancashire
Hot Pot and Shepherd's Pie were originally mutton dishes and
illustrate well the Northern skill of making the most of limited
ingredients and resources.

Mutton in its original form is now found in many speciality
foods. In Cumbria, remote enough to repel the advances of
technology, Herdwick sheep are still farmed for their strong,
sweet mutton hams. Mutton pies, sweetened with currants,
raisins, sultanas, apples, almonds and brown sugar, are also
produced by some of the more traditional sheep farmers.

> ASHDOWN SMOKERS, Skellerah Farm, Corney, Millom, Cumberland
> Telephone: 065 78 324
> Herdwick lamb hams, which Ashdown call 'Herdwick Macon', are a unique Cumbrian speciality, dry-cured and smoked over juniper and oak. The Herdwick Macon is distributed all over the UK through wholesalers and is also available on the Continent in various specialist food outlets. To find out exactly where in the UK and Europe you can find Herdwick Macon, as well as other Ashdown products, contact Harry Fellows at Skellerah Farm.

Britain has long been famed for its meat pies, both hot and cold, with the widest variety of fillings imaginable. During Medieval times, savoury and sweet fillings were mixed almost indiscriminately and the pastry case was invariably glazed with sugar. In Northern regions, hot meat pies provided an entire meal for the working populace, bought from pie shops, where they were baked on the premises using local meat and, if the meat was of mediocre quality, lots of spices to disguise its flavour.

Different to pies anywhere else in the country, the hot meat pie of Lancashire is still sold in shops across the county, which open at lunchtime and again between 4.00 pm and 6.30 pm for 'tea-time'.

> WALTER HOLLAND & SONS, Baxenden, Accrington, Lancashire
> Telephone: 0706 213591
> As far as the many fans in the North-West of England are concerned, little has changed over the past 140 years at Hollands. Their pies and puddings are still delivered daily in liveried vehicles to fish and chip shops throughout the region and their quality is as consistently good as ever. So good, in fact, that when people leave Lancashire for elsewhere in the country, or even the world, they find that the thing they miss most is a Hollands pie.
> Go to any fish and chip shop in the Accrington area and the meat pies are sure to be supplied by Hollands.

Approximately 2½ million litres of milk per year are produced in Yorkshire, Cumbria and Lancashire. As not all of this can be bottled, farmers are eager to find profitable means of diversification, such as butter and cream making. CHEESE has been a successful industry in the north for centuries, with many of the larger national concerns, such as Dairy Crest, running businesses in the region.

LANCASHIRE

A semi-soft, crumbly, loose-textured cheese with a distinctive buttery taste, Lancashire cheese was traditionally made by farmers between the Rivers Ribble and Lune.

Until 1910, when additional starter was permitted, Lancashire cheese was always made with evening milk, ripened overnight and mixed with the morning's milk. The cheese varied considerably across the county, according to the farm, the weather, the pasture and the cheesemaker him- or, more often, herself.

The first commercial dairy making Lancashire cheese was established in Chipping in 1913. As the methods were complex and long, the scale of the dairy remained quite small. In 1939, there were 202 farms producing 1260 tons of unpasteurised Lancashire cheese, with dairy production bringing the total figure up to 4800 tons.

> LANCASHIRE CHEESEMAKERS
>
> Please telephone to make appointments to visit
> AMBROSE HALL FARM, Catforth Hall, Woodplumpton
> Telephone: 0772 690111
>
> T & J M BUTLER, Lower Barker Farm, Inglewhite, Preston
> Telephone: 0995 40334
>
> JOHN KIRKHAM, Beesley Farm, Mill Lane, Goosnargh, Preston
> Telephone: 0772 865335

THE DALES CHEESES

Cistercian monks settling in the Yorkshire Dales after 1066 discovered that local sheep's milk made excellent cheese, not unlike their own French Roquefort. They applied French cheese-making techniques, such as mixing the summer milk of Wensleydale ewes and mould ripening with local stone, to produce some outstanding creamy cheeses from their abbeys at Jervaulx, Fountains and Rievaulx.

The cheeses' fame (and the monks' techniques) spread northwards into Swaledale and Teesdale and east into Cleveland. The monks travelled out to farms lying on monastery land to teach the art of cheesemaking, with the finished cheeses forming part of the farmers' rent to the Church.

Following the dissolution of the monasteries, cheesemaking traditions remained with those farmers who had been taught so well by the monks. As demand increased, however, many farmers had to supplement their flocks with cattle in order to produce sufficient milk and eventually most of the Dales cheeses were made from cows' milk or, at best, a mixture of cows' and ewes' milk.

Today, many Dales farmers are adopting traditional Dales cheesemaking techniques and developing new varieties, often unpasteurised and invariably delicious. BOTTON CREAMERY in Danby, Yorkshire, produces DANBYDALE, an unpasteurised, semi-soft cheese with a crust made with milk from organically-managed herds.

And from Richmond in West Yorkshire, the Reeds produce the highly successful SWALEDALE, again unpasteurised and from organically-managed herds. Swaledale is a full-fat, semi-soft cheese and available from cheese factors all over the UK.

DAVID & MANDY REED, 29 Racecourse Road, Richmond, West Yorkshire
Telephone: 0748 824044/824932

WENSLEYDALE

The making of Wensleydale cheese begins in mid-May, with the very first products of the season being known as 'grass cheese', mid-season products as 'pasture cheese' and products made from the oldest grass or hay as 'fog cheese'. The season officially ends with the first frost.

Although most Wensleydale in production at present is white, it was traditionally a blue cheese, naturally mould-ripened.

WENSLEYDALE CHEESEMAKERS

Please telephone to make appointments to visit.

REDESDALE DAIRY, Soppitt Farm, Otterburn, Northumberland
Telephone: 0830 20506 – unpasteurised, from Ayrshire cow's milk and Friesian ewe's milk
Also made at dairy:
NORTH TYNDALE • (unpasteurised, cow's milk)
COQUETDALE • (unpasteurised, mould-ripened)
REDESDALE • (unpasteurised, ewe's milk)

FOUNTAINS DAIRY, Kirkby Malzeard, Ripon, Yorkshire
Telephone: 076 583 212/495 – pasteurised, available all year
Also made at dairy: COVERDALE • (pasteurised, semi-hard, white)

Of course, not all northern cheesemakers are following in the footsteps of the ancient monks. Many are branching out in newer directions, producing wonderful cheeses from the milk of goats and ewes. There are also numerous highly acclaimed modern cow's milk cheeses being produced in the north.

Please telephone to arrange to visit the following cheesemakers.

ASHES FARM, Horton in Ribblesdale, Settle, Yorkshire
Telephone: 07296 231
• Ribblesdale Goat Cheese – pasteurised. Also available smoked and with sage.

CALTHWAITE DAIRY, Penrith, Cumbria
Telephone: 076 885 292
• Calthwaite – Jersey cow's milk cheese, low-fat, soft

COLLEGE FARMS DAIRY, Higher College Farm, Hothersall, Longridge, Preston, Lancashire
Telephone: 077478 3604/5182
• Ribchester – goat's milk cheese, also available smoked

THORNBY MOOR DAIRY, Thornby Moor House, Aikton, Wigton, Cumbria
Telephone: 0965 43160
• Allendale – unpasteurised, full-fat, hard
• Bewcastle – unpasteurised, hard
• Cumberland Farmhouse – unpasteurised, full-fat, hard, also available smoked and with herbs.

Wensleydale

HIGH TEA

During the 19th century, at around 4.00 pm, upper and middle class society took afternoon tea consisting of delicate sandwiches and elegant cakes and biscuits, to stave off their hunger until dinner later in the evening.

In the working class areas of the North, however, 'dinner' was eaten around midday and the following meal, in the evening, was called 'high tea'. Far more substantial than the Southern afternoon tea, it was an entire meal, made up of pies, rich fruit cakes, tarts, scones, hams, potted meat and fish dishes, savouries and biscuits.

Following the conquest of India in the mid 18th century, combined with vigorous propaganda by the now British-owned East India Company, tea ousted beer as Britain's most popular drink and invariably accompanied this vast feast.

A visit to the Northern cities of York and Harrogate would not be complete without tea, small or large, at Bettys. The original Bettys tea-shop was established in Harrogate in 1919 by a Swiss confectioner, who had the bright idea of applying Swiss culinary techniques to traditional Yorkshire recipes. Today, there are around 400 different types of cake from which to choose, including rich fruit cake accompanied by Wensleydale cheese. A wide variety of teas and coffees is also available.

BETTYS, 1 Parliament Street, Harrogate, North Yorkshire
Telephone: 0423 502746

BETTYS, St. Helen's Square, York, North Yorkshire
Telephone: 0904 59142

OLD PECULIAR CAKE

6 fl oz/170 ml/¾ cup Theakstons Old Peculiar ale
9 oz/250 g/1 cup currants
9 oz/250 g/1 cup sultanas
9 oz/250 g/1 cup raisins
4½ oz/125 g/½ cup red cherries
6 oz/170 g/¾ cup mixed peel
9 oz/250 g/1 cup butter
9 oz/250 g/1 cup caster sugar
3 eggs, beaten
9 oz/250 g/1¾ cups flour, sieved
3½ oz/100 g/½ cup walnut halves

walnut halves, for decoration

Soak dried fruit in Old Peculiar ale overnight prior to making. Preheat oven to 170°C/325°F/Gas Mark 3. Place the butter and sugar in a bowl and cream together. Gradually add the egg a little at a time, scraping down the bowl after each addition. Finally stir in the fruit, flour, nuts and mix well. This mixture is sufficient to fill an 8 in/20 cm square or a 9 in/22.5 cm round cake tin. Pour the mixture into greased, lined tins and level off evenly. Decorate the top with walnuts. Bake for 2¾–3 hours, until a skewer inserted in the centre comes out clean.

(BETTYS)

YORKSHIRE TEACAKE

½ oz/15 g/2 tbs fresh yeast
8 fl oz/225 ml/1 cup lukewarm milk
12 oz/340 g/2½ cups white bread flour
1½ oz/42 g/1 tbs lard
pinch salt
pinch caster sugar
1½ oz/42 g/1½ tbs currants
pinch of mixed spice

Dissolve the yeast in luke warm milk. Place the flour into a bowl with the lard and rub in to form a fine crumb. Add the salt, sugar, currants and spice and mix well. Make a well in the centre of the flour and pour in the yeast mixture. Sprinkle a little of the flour over the surface, cover the bowl and leave in a warm place until frothy. Remove the cover and work the liquid into the flour, forming a dough. Turn onto a lightly floured surface and knead until the dough is smooth. Weigh off the dough into 3 oz/85 g/½ cup pieces. Roll each piece into a ball, and using a rolling pin flatten each ball into a flat round, about a third of an inch thick. Place onto a greased baking tray. Cover and leave in a warm place to rise. When well risen place into the oven at 200°C/400°F/Gas Mark 6 for 10–15 minutes until golden brown. The final appearance can be enhanced by brushing with a boiled solution of sugar and water (½ pt/300 ml/1 cup water plus 4 oz/110 g/½ cup granulated sugar), boiled for 3 minutes. Brush this over the surface of each teacake while still warm, to give a glossy appearance.

(BETTYS)

Originally, GINGERBREAD was much thinner and harder than that baked today. It was a development of unleavened bread, made with breadcrumbs, ginger, liquorice, aniseed, pepper and honey. Flour, eggs and fat replaced many of these ingredients, followed soon after by the addition of sugar and treacle, to produce the more familiar thick, moist biscuit.

Most regions of Britain can boast their own particular type of gingerbread. Many Northern gingerbreads use oatmeal rather than wheat-flour and are known as parkin. Both Yorkshire and Lancashire have their own parkin recipes and even these differ according to the town from which they originate.

Grasmere Gingerbread from Westmoreland uses flour, almonds and golden syrup amongst its ingredients; its true recipe is such a closely guarded secret, however, that nobody know for sure how it should really be made.

> At the Gingerbread Shop in Grasmere, gingerbread is baked daily on the site of the old village school, as it has been for the past 135 years. Grasmere gingerbread cannot be bought anywhere else except from the shop and again, the recipe is a secret.
>
> THE GINGERBREAD SHOP, Church Cottage, Grasmere, Cumbria
> Telephone: 09665 428
> Opening times: Mid-February to mid-November 9.30 am to 4.30 pm every day of the week. Best to telephone first.

Many Northern cakes and puddings were originally reliant on oatmeal, making them somewhat heavy. During the 18th century, however, ports such as Maryport, Workington and Whitehaven in Cumbria did considerable trade with the West Indies, importing rum, brown sugar, lemons, oranges and spices. These, together with the arrival of raising agents, gave much-needed sweetness and levity to many local cakes and desserts.

BREWING

Barley being well suited to Northern soils, there is a strong and well-established brewing tradition across most of the region. Nowhere else in England is there such a wide variety of beers on offer but one thing is insisted upon in pubs and working men's social clubs throughout the region – a full head of foam on top.

The most famous brown ale of them all (and there are a lot in the North) comes from Newcastle; Newcastle Brown, brewed by The Tyne Brewery, is now popular all over Britain and available not only in pubs but also in cans and bottles in off-licence outlets.

Four sturdy grey stone bridges span the Beck at Clapham in North Yorkshire

> THE TYNE BREWERY, Gallowgate, Newcastle-upon-Tyne
> Telephone: 091 232 5091
> Tours around the Tyne Brewery are available on request. As well as seeing the famous Newcastle Brown being brewed, visitors may also see the other beers produced by Newcastle Breweries, including the highly acclaimed Theakston Best Bitter.

REAL ALE

To qualify, as far as aficionados are concerned at least, as 'real ale', the beer in question must have been conditioned in its cask. The quality and flavour of real ale comes to being during its secondary fermentation, taking place in the cask itself rather than in a bottle, like wine.

Brewing requires high specification barley – high in starch and low in nitrogen – in order that the sugars can be easily extracted. There is relatively little barley grown in this country which satisfies these demands, hence the rarity value accorded to real ales. There are literally hundreds of real ales produced in the north of England alone; each region has its own specialities and some operations are so specialised that they only supply to one or two pubs in a nearby town.

In the North-East, for example, they like their ale to be malty and light and Vaux Breweries of Sunderland produce LORIMER'S BEST SCOTCH to satisfy that demand. But you only have to travel a little further south, into Teeside, to find much stronger real ales, such as CAMERON'S STRONGARM.

Yorkshire has gained such a reputation for its real ales that many beers originating from the county are given the appellation 'Yorkshire bitter', an indication of their quality. As well as massive concerns like SAMUEL SMITH and JOSHUA TETLEY, Yorkshire is also home to some highly esoteric brews, like THE BIG END BREWERY in Harrogate, who only supply two pubs.

For those determined to seek out the wierd and wonderful, Roger Protz's pocket-sized *Real Ale Drinker's Almanac* (Lochar, £6.99) is indispensable.

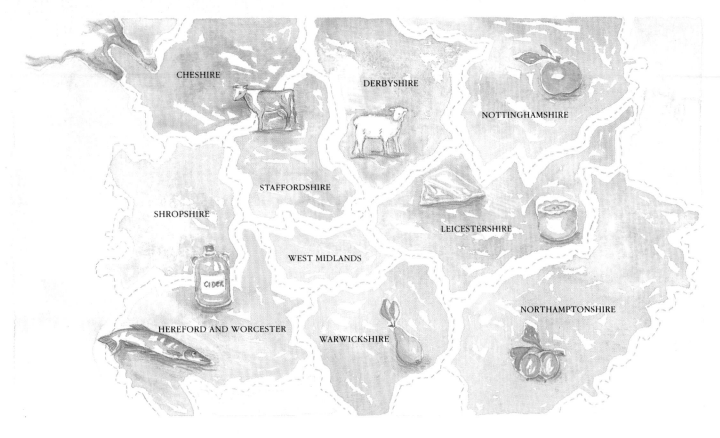

THE MIDLANDS

SOME of Britain's richest agricultural land is to be found in the southern part of the Midlands, particularly in HEREFORD and WORCESTER.

The VALE OF EVESHAM is recognised as one of Britain's foremost fruit-growing regions. Soft fruits like black and redcurrants, gooseberries and blackberries thrive, and orchards of apple and pear trees cover the fields of the Vale; in Herefordshire, the apples are not all destined for cooking or eating – many are made into famous Hereford cider, the great rival to West Country cider and quite different in taste and aroma.

The apple orchards blossom in the Spring and by Autumn, the branches are weighed down with cider apples, ready for harvesting. Little has changed in terms of basic cider making techniques, although some of the machinery has made life a little easier. The apples are still washed and pulped and the juice pressed. Yeast is added to the juice and the mixture is fermented in huge oak vats, where it remains to mature. Finally, to produce the different styles of cider – dry, medium, sweet, still, sparkling – different varieties of cider apples are blended.

One of the many bountiful apple orchards in the Vale of Evesham

The Cider Museum in Hereford

H. P. BULMER plc, The Cider Mills, Plough Lane, Hereford
Telephone: 0432 352000
H. P. Bulmer was established in 1887 by Percy Bulmer, son of a
Herefordshire vicar who took apples from the rectory orchard
and pressed them in a cider mill on a nearby farm. He produced a
few thousand gallons of cider before opening his first proper mill
in Ryegate Street. The modern Bulmer's mill still surrounds the
original one, now producing one of Britain's most successful
ranges of cider, as well as a selection of other internationally
recognised drinks.

THE CIDER MUSEUM, Hereford
Telephone: 0432 354207
Not only the history of Herefordshire cider but cider from all
over the world.
Open from April to October every day of the week 10.00 am to
5.30 pm.
Open from November to Easter Monday to Saturday 1.00 pm to
5.00 pm.

The Pershore plum, a yellow plum particularly suited to
cooking, was first discovered growing in a wood in Pershore in
the Vale of Evesham. Pears are also widely grown and are used
for another traditional Hereford sideline, perry, the production
process for which is almost identical to that for cider, with pears
replacing the cider apples.

Most fruit growers in the area offer Pick-Your-Own facilities but it
is advisable to telephone first. These include:

DINMORE FRUIT FARM, Hereford, Hereford & Worcester
Telephone: 056 884 361
17 varieties of apple and 3 varieties of pear, strawberries,
raspberries, blackberries, apple juice, herbs, vegetables

PAUL DUNSBY & SONS, Cotswold Orchards, Broadway,
Worcestershire
Telephone: 0356 3142
Apples – Cox's Orange Pippin, Egremont Russett, Bramley's
Seedling

VALE PLUMS LTD., Dunnington Heath Farm, Dunnington,
Alcester, Warwickshire
Telephone: 0929 772771
Dessert plums – Victoria, Swan, Heron, Damsons, Marjorie
Seedlings.

GREEN ACRES ORGANIC FRUIT AND VEGETABLES, Dinmore,
Hereford & Worcester
Telephone: 056884 7045
30 types of organically-grown fruit and vegetables, picked daily

An old poster from The Cider Museum

WILD WOOD PIGEON WITH LOVAGE

1 fl oz/30 ml/2 tbs sunflower oil
6 plump wild wood pigeons
1 medium sized onion, chopped
few fresh lovage leaves
3 pts/1.7 litres/6 cups dry perry
1 oz/28 g/1 tbs cornflour
1 oz/28 g/1 tbs tamari
sea salt
freshly ground black pepper

Heat the oven to 150°C/300°F/Gas Mark 2. Heat the oil in a
large frying pan and brown the breasts of the pigeons.
Remove from the heat and fit them head-end down in a
casserole. Sprinkle with the chopped onions, tuck in the
lovage leaves and pour in the perry to cover. Cover with a
lid. Cook in the oven for about 2½–3 hours, until the breasts
are tender. Drain off most of the juice and keep the pigeons
warm while you prepare the sauce.

Strain the remaining cooking juice into a saucepan and
reduce over a high heat to approximately ¾ pt/425 ml/1½ cups.
Taste and add a few more lovage leaves if necessary. Thicken
the sauce slightly with the cornflour. Strain through a fine
sieve and season with the tamari and salt and pepper.

Carve the breasts off the pigeons and return to the warm
liquid. Keep the remaining parts of the bird to make stock for
a game soup. To serve, quickly drain each pigeon breast on a
piece of absorbent kitchen paper and arrange on a warm
serving plate, surrounded by the sauce. Garnish with a few
lovage leaves.

Serves 6
(PATRICIA HEGARTY AT HOPE END)

BAKEWELL in Derbyshire is best known for its Bakewell pudding, now recognised and loved all over Britain. Popular culture would have it that the first Bakewell pudding was made by accident, when a cook at the Rutland Arms in Bakewell misunderstood the instructions of her mistress. The story goes that in 1860 another local cook heard how well the 'wrong' puddings were received and stole the recipe, making the puddings herself on the site of what is now The Olde Original Bakewell Pudding Shop. Despite this, very similar puddings are recorded a century earlier, served as sweetmeats or under the name Duke of Cambridge pudding at the beginning of the 19th century.

BAKEWELL PUDDING

8 oz/225 g/1 cup puff pastry
2 eggs
4 oz/110 g/½ cup butter
6 oz/170 g/½ cup raspberry jam
2 oz/56 g/⅓ cup sugar

Heat oven to 180°C/350°F/Gas Mark 4. Line a greased tart mould with the pastry and cover with a layer of jam. Melt the butter, then take pan off heat and stir in the egg, add the sugar and beat well. Pour into the tart mould. Bake in the oven until delicately brown.

Serves 4
(THE LYGON ARMS)

A sumptuous range of summer produce on sale at a roadside stall in Wickhamford near Evesham

Each county or even town in the Midlands seems to boast its own special type of cake or biscuit. Many of these adopted the name of their town in order to be noticed at the many fairs which used to take place across the region. Back in the 13th century, the Nottingham Goose Fair was originally a meeting place for farmers to trade their Michaelmas Geese and eventually attracted all sorts of food producers, selling Shrewsbury biscuits, brandy snaps and little raised gooseberry pies. The Goose Fair, now a huge fun-fair, still takes place every year, but a goose is a rare sight.

THE OLDE ORIGINAL BAKEWELL PUDDING SHOP, The Square, Bakewell, Derbyshire
Telephone: 062981 2193
Open every day of the year, 9.00 am to 5.00 pm

The Olde Original Bakewell Pudding shop stands on the same site on which the first puddings were baked in 1860

For something a little more luxurious, try CALLOW HALL in Derbyshire, one of the nation's top country house hotels. Built in the 19th century and set in beautifully wooded grounds, service is old fashioned and the atmosphere is sedately elegant.

The Hall also houses its own bakery and patisserie, run by the owners, who have been bakers for centuries. Food is taken very seriously indeed; all meat is butchered on the premises and carefully hung.

CALLOW HALL, Mappleton Road, Ashbourne, Derbyshire
Telephone: 0335 43403

During the 18th and 19th centuries, the staple Midlands crop was oats but barley and winter wheat have now taken over as the most widely-grown crops in the region. However, many dishes making use of oats have survived as a very important part of the local culinary heritage. For example, crumpets and pikelets are now popular all over Britain.

PIKELETS

8 oz/225 g/3 cups strong white flour
4 g/1 tsp salt
½ oz/15 g/2 tsp yeast
¼ pt/150 ml/½ cup warm milk
¼ pt/150 ml/½ cup warm water
1 g/¼ tsp bicarbonate of soda
4 tbs/60 ml/¼ cup cold water
1 egg white, lightly beaten

Sieve flour and salt together into a bowl. Dissolve the yeast with the warm milk and water and pour into the flour. Beat mixture vigorously for 5 minutes to make a smooth batter. Cover with a cloth and allow to prove for about 30 minutes in a warm place. Dissolve the bicarbonate of soda in the cold water and beat into the batter. Fold in the beaten egg white. Lightly grease a griddle or heavy based frying pan. Put a tablespoon of mixture onto the hot surface and cook until the pikelet is no longer wet. Turn over and cook until the other side is lightly browned. Continue until all the batter is used.

Makes 12

(THE LYGON ARMS)

Oatcakes are almost taken for granted in Staffordshire, where they have been enjoyed by rich and poor alike since the mid 18th century; further afield, however, they are only just being noticed. Cooked on a griddle each day at numerous bakeries and shops across the county, oatcakes are usually eaten for breakfast at the weekend with any combination of cheese, bacon, mushrooms, tomatoes, eggs and black pudding.

NORTH STAFFS OATCAKE BAKERS, Turner Crescent, Chesterton, Newcastle-under-Lyme, Staffordshire
Telephone: 0782 562804
Established 35 years ago, North Staffs Oatcake Bakers have earned the accolade of being the first oatcake bakers in the region to have been asked to supply London. Neal's Yard, one of the capital's foremost speciality food shops, have now been selling North Staffs oatcakes for around 18 months. Meanwhile, the bakery has continued to supply traditional oatcakes, made with local oatmeal and wheatgerm and cooked on hot-plates, to supermarkets and shops all around Staffordshire.

In much of the rural Midlands, farmers worked hand in hand with the textile-rich industrial areas, breeding sheep for their wool rather than their meat. Some mutton and lamb sheep are still bred in Hereford & Worcester and Derbyshire, enjoying the sheltered valleys and long grass, but in general, cattle and pigs are more prolific.

THE HEREFORD COW

A cross between a British Red Longhorn and cattle from the Low Countries, the Hereford is one of the oldest English breeds and arguably the first, dating back to the 17th century.

Until the 18th century it was a different animal – much smaller and tougher than today, but then Leicestershire farmer Robert Bakewell developed the modern red and white breed, a

The Hereford Cow is one of England's oldest breeds of cattle

common sight in the fields of Hereford and Worcester.

It is remarkably healthy, strong enough to breed outside in early Spring and to ward off many of the diseases to which other cattle often fall prey. It feeds on the lush grasslands, maturing early to give succulent beef.

CASSEROLED OXTAIL IN
SAVOY CABBAGE LEAVES

2 lb 7 oz/2 kg oxtail pieces
2 oz/56 g/1½ tbs dripping
7 oz/200 g/1¼ cup onion, diced
3 oz/225 g/¾ cup carrot, diced
3½ oz/100 g/¾ cup celery, diced
3½ pts/2 litres/7 cups beef jus (jus is greatly reduced stock)
2 oz/56 g/1½ tbs tomato puree
1 bay leaf
3 parsley stalks
5 juniper berries
1 sprig of fresh thyme
½ bottle/365 ml/1¼ cups red wine
2 savoy cabbages, approx. 4 lb 7 oz–5 lb 5 oz/2–2.5 kg
40 baby carrots
3 oz/85 g crispy bacon julienne
8 oz/225 g/1 cup mashed potato
1 egg yolk
8 fl oz/225 g/1 cup double cream

Heat oven to 180°C/350°F/Gas Mark 4. In a heavy bottomed pan, melt the dripping and when very hot, add the oxtail and brown all over. Remove from the pan and put to one side. To the pan, add the diced onion, carrot and celery and cook until golden brown. Add the tomato puree and lightly roast. Deglaze with the red wine and reduce down by about a quarter. Put the oxtail back into the pan. Pour on the beef jus and simmer. Skim away all the grease. Add the bayleaf, juniper berries, peppercorns, parsley stalks and thyme. Cover with a lid and braise in the oven for 3 hours.

When the meat is soft and comes easily away from the bone, remove the pan from the oven and allow to cool slightly. Remove the oxtail and strip the meat from the bones and cover the meat with a damp cloth. Pour the liquid into a clean pan through a sieve and reduce until quite thick.

Take the outside leaves from the cabbage leaving them whole. Cook them in boiling water until soft. Refresh in iced water and drain well on a cloth. Remove all the stalks from the cabbage leaves and line souffle dishes with the leaves, leaving no gaps.

Julienne the remaining cabbage and cook with a little butter in a pan with a tight fitting lid until very soft. Season and allow to cool. Peel and lightly boil the baby carrots. Mix the oxtail with a little of the beef jus and divide between the 8 moulds evenly. Divide most of the julienne of cabbage between the 8 moulds. Fold over the leaves to enclose the cabbage and oxtail. Place the mashed potato in a pan, mix in the remaining cabbage and cook until hot. Whisk together egg yolk and cream and place a little on the potato mix. To serve, heat the moulds in a steamer until the oxtail is hot. Reheat the carrots, toss in butter and season. Reheat the beef jus and check the seasoning. Turn the mould out onto the front half of each plate. Glaze the potato mixture under the grill. Position the potato at 1400 hours and the carrots at 2200 hours. Each plate should contain 8 carrots. Pour a ring of jus around each plate and serve immediately.

Serves 8
(DAVID DORRICOTT AT THE PORTMAN
INTERCONTINENTAL HOTEL, LONDON)

FORDHALL ORGANIC FARM, Market Drayton, Shropshire
Telephone: 0630 83255
Arthur Hollins has been farming organically for over 40 years. All his animals, including cows, sheep, pigs and poultry, feed on a permanent pasture of around 40 different types of grass, herbs, wild flowers and plants. Only when the weather is particularly severe is the animals' diet supplemented by feed such as hay.

The farm is watered by carefully-controlled local supplies as well as by Fordhall's own springs.

In addition to selling a range of Soil Association approved products in the farm shop, Arthur is a crusader for environmentally-sound farming methods. He has developed a relatively simple system of ploughing which does not disturb the natural balance of the soil and produces healthier crops and plants. He also lectures in America and Europe on organic farming techniques.

MOORS FARM AND COUNTRY RESTAURANT, Chillington Lane, Codsall, Near Wolverhampton, Staffordshire
Telephone: 09074 2330
Fresh produce from Moors Farm makes up the menu in the small restaurant. There is also a shop selling fruit, potatoes, poultry, eggs, jams, cakes and pickles – again, all produced on the farm. Please telephone to book for dinner or to visit the farm.

British cooking is famous for its great variety of meat pies

As in many of the Northern counties of England, pork has a special place in the culinary history of the Midlands, with a wide variety of traditional pork products to be found. Again, many of these quality products are the result of past hardships, being economical to produce and satisfying to eat.

In addition to the MELTON MOWBRAY variety, there are many versions of the pork pie, some to be eaten hot, most eaten cold. Original pork pies were hand-raised, the crust or 'coffyn' hand-moulded round a wooden shape. Leicestershire is one of the most prolific pork pie producing counties, with different pies emanating from different towns and villages across the county.

THE HUNT

Two of Britain's most famous hunts, the Quorn and the Belvoir, have pursued the fox over the Shires for centuries.

Thundering over hedgerows and fields creates an enormous appetite and many satisfying and delicious foods have become associated with the hunt. Some, like the Melton Hunt Cake, rich with fruit and sherry, were reserved for those in red coats, while attendants with the Quorn were given suet pudding wrapped around bacon, seasoned with herbs and sweetened with syrup.

The Melton Mowbray pork pie, now famous throughout the country, was originally served as the hunt passed through Melton Mowbray and was soon being requested in London. For a true Melton Mowbray pie, the hot-water crust should be made with lard and glazed egg, so that it turns golden brown when baked. The filling should be of prime pork, two parts lean to one part fat, seasoned with salt and pepper. Pork bone jelly is poured in at the end.

DICKINSON AND MORRIS, 10 Nottingham Street, Melton Mowbray, Leicestershire
Telephone: 0664 62341
Traditional Melton Mowbray pork pies, made to a 100 year-old recipe.
Traditional Melton Hunt Cake.

WORCESTERSHIRE SAUCE

To accompany many of the meat and game dishes of the Midlands there are several strong, spicy sauces. This may be a sharp onion sauce with stewed pheasant or a mustard and garlic sauce with wild rabbit. Strong sauces as an accompaniment are not always quite so complex – bottled sauces such as tomato ketchup or fruit and spice sauce are seen on many kitchen tables to go with meat dishes. But of all the bottled sauces, Worcestershire sauce must surely be the most famous.

However, Worcestershire sauce did not begin life very successfully in Britain. Lord Sandys of Worcester, an ex-Governor of Bengal, returned from India with a recipe for his favourite Indian sauce and asked local chemists John Lea and William Perrins to reproduce it for him.

The result was so dreadful that the sauce was abandoned in the cellar. When it was found by chance several months later and tasted again, it had matured into a truly delicious spicy sauce.

Worcestershire sauce is still made by Lea and Perrins in Worcester to its original recipe and left to mature in hogshead for several months before bottling.

LEA AND PERRINS LTD, 3 Midland Road, Worcester
Telephone: 0905 763367

WORCESTERSHIRE HERB SOUP

1 large onion, chopped
1 oz/28 g/1 tbs butter
2 pts/1.2 litres/4 cups stock from a cooked ham joint
2 heads of lettuce
8 oz/225 g/2 cups sorrel
2 heads of chicory
4 cloves
a pinch of ground mace
2 oz/56 g/¼ cup chopped sweet herbs (e.g. basil, tarragon, chervil, borage, parsley)
8–12 asparagus tips
salt and pepper, to taste

Saute the onion in the butter, until soft. Add the stock and bring to the boil. Simmer and add the lettuce, sorrel, chicory, cloves and mace. Cook for 20 minutes. Puree and sieve. Add the sweet herbs and the asparagus tips. Season to taste. Reheat gently and serve.

Serves 4
(THE LYGON ARMS)

The rolling pastures of Shropshire, Staffordshire, Derbyshire and Cheshire are perfect for the production of milk, with the right blend of warmth and moisture. In fact, this is the biggest milk producing region in Britain, and an ideal area for cheese-making.

CHEESE AND LEEK SOUFFLE

1 oz/28 g/1 tbs butter
2 oz/56 g/½ cup leeks, very finely diced
3 oz/85 g/1 cup Stilton cheese
2 eggs
7 fl oz/200 ml/1 cup double cream
salt and pepper, to taste

Heat the oven to 180°C/375°F/Gas Mark 5. Melt butter in a thick bottomed pan and add the diced leeks. Cover with buttered greaseproof paper and cook very gently until soft. The natural juices from the leek will give enough liquid for cooking. Crumble the Stilton into two greased individual souffle dishes. Whisk the whole eggs and cream together well. Stir in the leeks and season well. Pour the egg and cream mixture onto the cheese in the dishes and place onto a flat baking tray. Bake in the oven for 20–25 minutes until golden brown and firm to touch. Serve immediately.

Serves 2
(DAVID DORRICOTT AT THE PORTMAN INTERCONTINENTAL HOTEL, LONDON)

Cheese and Leek Souffle

Blue Stilton – the King of Cheeses

BLUE STILTON

The first records of Blue Stilton, the King of Cheeses, date back to the early 18th century, when a farmer's wife living near Melton Mowbray, Leicestershire sold cheese made on the farm to travellers staying at her brother-in-law's coaching house in the town of Stilton, Cambridgeshire.

By the end of the century, the cheese had become so popular that the recipe, or at least versions of it, had spread to all the small dairies in the region; factory production began in 1870 to produce Blue Stilton on the larger scale it was now demanding.

In 1910, however, cheesemakers saw that unless action was taken, Blue Stilton would become lost in a maze of variations. Its territory was therefore defined and all Stilton cheese had to be made from milk taken from cows living in the Vale of Belvoir. In 1969, the British government gave Stilton the protection of law, defining it as: "A blue or white cheese made with full cream milk with no applied pressure, forming its own crust or coat and made in cylindrical form, the milk coming from English dairy herds in the district of Melton Mowbray and surrounding areas".

The Stilton Cheesemakers' Association, set up in 1936, now has six members, all of whom conform to the original definition and are allowed to display the unique Stilton trademark.

STILTON CHEESEMAKERS

J. M. NUTTALL & CO, Dove Dairy, Hartington, Buxton, Derbyshire SK17 0AH
Telephone: 0298 84496
Blue and white Stilton; also YE OLDE CHEESE SHOPPE – with a capacity to store 90,000 cheeses and a wide range of British farmhouse cheeses on sale

WEBSTER'S DAIRY LTD., Saxelbye, Melton Mowbray, Leicestershire
Telephone: 0664 812223
Blue and white Stilton made in 100 year-old dairy

TUXFORD AND TEBBUTT, Thorpe End, Melton Mowbray, Leicestershire LE13 1RE
Telephone: 0664 500555
Blue Stilton; also famed for their Red Leicester

COLSTON BASSETT AND DISTRICT DAIRY, Colston Bassett, Nottinghamshire NG12 3FM
Telephone: 0949 81322
Unpasteurised matured Stilton

LONG CLAWSON DAIRY, Long Clawson, Melton Mowbray, Leicestershire
Telephone: 0664 822332
Blue and white Stilton – *no visitors*

MILLWAY FOODS LTD., Colston Lane, Harby, Nr. Melton Mowbray, Leicestershire
Telephone: 0949 61371

STILTON CHEESEMAKERS ASSOCIATION
Telephone: 0298 26224

RED LEICESTER

Red Leicester, a rich, semi-hard flaky cheese, originates in Gloucester and was not recorded in Leicestershire until the late 16th century. As it matures, its flavour becomes nuttier and a blue mould develops on its surface. It is now the sole survivor of the original Shire cheeses.

White Leicester came about as a result of an aversion amongst dairyists and cheesemakers to added colourant of any kind but modern Leicester cheesemakers add annatto, a natural colouring derived from the seed pods of a tropical tree.

CHESHIRE

Cheshire, a hard, crumbling white cheese, was originally made all over the Midlands and only became peculiar to the county when Derbyshire and Leicestershire developed their own cheeses. It is, in fact, the oldest of all the British cheeses and is recorded as having been on sale in the markets of Ancient

Rome. It was quick to become highly-prized in London – Ye Olde Cheshire Cheese pub in Fleet Street served it with ale and fruit cake.

The secret to the distinctive flavour of Cheshire cheese lies in the salinity of the rock on which the fields of Cheshire are laid. The salt seeps through into the pastureland which is in turn grazed by Cheshire cattle. Strictly speaking, the milk should remain unpasteurised, allowing each cheese's individual flavour to reflect the season in which the milk was taken.

The finely-marbled appearance of Blue Cheshire comes about through longer maturation – it is quite rare and strong in flavour and should be stored with care.

CHESHIRE CHEESEMAKERS

HENRY BARNETT & SONS, Overton Hall, Malpas, Cheshire SY14 7DG
Telephone: 0948 860519
Traditional unpasteurised Cheshire, red and white

APPLEBY'S OF HAWKSTONE, Hawkstone Abbey Farm, Weston-under-Redcastle, Shrewsbury, Shropshire
Telephone: 0948 840387
Red and white Cheshire

HUTCHINSON SMITH & SON, Hinton Bank Farm, Whitchurch, Shropshire SY13 4HB
Telephone: 0948 2631
Blue-veined Cheshire cheese, unpasteurised

POTTED CHEESE

2 oz/56 g/¼ cup unsalted butter
2 oz/56 g/¼ cup grated Cheshire cheese
3½ fl oz/100 ml/¼ cup Port or cream sherry
cayenne pepper, to taste
clarified butter

Gently soften the butter. Combine with the grated cheese and all the other ingredients. Beat together into a smooth paste. Press into small pots and cover with a film of clarified butter. To clarify butter, put required amount of butter in a small pan and warm it very slowly. When all the sediment has dropped to the bottom, carefully pour off the clear butter.

BEER

As in the Northern counties, there is a well-established tradition of beer drinking in the Midlands, almost as strong today as it was centuries ago before tea overtook ale as Britain's most popular drink.

'Mild' is a low-gravity beer of particular popularity in the Midlands. Usually cheaper than bitter, it is treated with great reverence in Midlands cities such as Stoke-on-Trent and Birmingham, where it is served in a straight-sided glass.

Burton-on-Trent in Staffordshire is generally agreed to be the capital of Britain's brewing towns, possessing 5 breweries which supply bitter and mild beers to local pubs and off-licences as well as for the rest of the country and for export. One of the region's favourite ales, Indian Pale Ale, was originally brewed for export to the colonies. It was not successful there but the Midlands beer drinkers took to it and now I.P.A. is available in pubs all over the nation.

BASS MUSEUM OF BREWING, Horninglow Street, Burton-on-Trent, Staffordshire
Telephone: 0283 511000
The museum houses traditional brewing equipment and interesting displays to illustrate brewing methods through the ages. There are also Shire horses kept in the stables and, if booked in advance, tours around the modern Bass brewery may be arranged.
Opening times: 10.00 am to 5.00 pm Monday to Friday
10.30 am to 5.00 pm Saturday and Sunday
Open every day of the year except Christmas

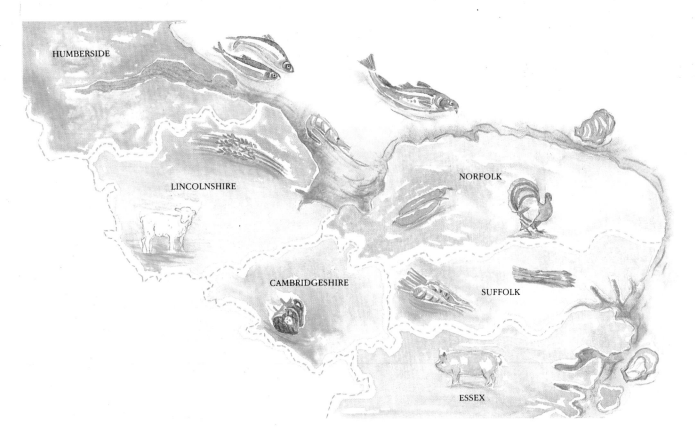

EAST ANGLIA

D RIVING along the seemingly endless lanes of rural East Anglia, fields uninterrupted by hedgerows, stretching out on either side as far as the eye can see, the unfamiliar visitor might assume that little could flourish in such exposed conditions. On the contrary, the land is blessed with exceptionally warm summers and dry winds, as well as a long coastline, making it one of England's most prosperous agricultural regions.

The gently rolling countryside of SUFFOLK is perfect for vines, hence the high proportion of English wines produced in the county. Its fields of rape and mustard seed slope away to the coast, where marsh samphire grows in abundance in the small, sheltered inlets.

NORFOLK, with its awesome windswept clifftops at its northern-most reaches is largely unspoilt and proud of its traditions – the villagers closely guard their way of life and visitors, while welcomed, are regarded with a measure of caution. Grey stone Norman churches squatting watchfully in even the smallest hamlets are a constant reminder that Norfolk

Sproughton Mill, Suffolk

was one of the first places encountered by the invading French in the 11th century.

The CAMBRIDGESHIRE countryside is flat and warm, with its fields fertile enough for crops, vegetables and soft fruits. Through the university town of CAMBRIDGE flows the River Cam, populated by punting students and visitors during the summer. Cambridge, perhaps more than Oxford, is a town thoroughly saturated by college life. As well as visiting Kings College and taking a punt along the Backs, visitors can take advantage of the wealth of excellent tea shops and coffee houses.

FITZBILLIES, at 52 Trumpington Street and 50 Regent Street, Cambridge
Telephone: 0223 352500
One of the town's best tea shops, serving traditional tea-time fare, as well as their famous Chelsea Buns. The recipe is a jealously guarded secret. Both tea shops are very busy during the summer but are worth queuing for.

CAMBRIDGE BURNT CREAM

This dish has been enjoyed since the 17th century but became particularly popular in Trinity College, Cambridge, in the late 19th century.

6 egg yolks
2 oz/56 g/2 tbs caster sugar
½ oz/15 g/4 tsp cornflour
1 pt/570 ml/2 cups double cream
a few drops of vanilla essence

Beat the egg yolks with the caster sugar and cornflour in a bowl until light and fluffy. Heat the cream and vanilla essence to just below boiling and remove from heat. Pour into the egg mixture, stirring continuously. Return the mixture to the saucepan and heat very gently until the sauce thickens – only a couple of minutes. Pour the custard mixture into small individual dishes and leave to cool, then chill. Cover each custard with an even layer of caster sugar and brown under a very hot grill. When the sugar has caramelised and is brown, remove from under the grill and let the caramel harden.

Serves 4

Moving further North into the vast tract of land that is LINCOLNSHIRE, the villages become less frequent and the landscape becomes seemingly more spartan. These enormous fields contain the largest proportion of Britain's root crops.

East Anglia has a long and varied coastline. This is great news for visitors – freshly-caught local fish are easy to seek out in restaurants, hotels and cafes as well as on fishmongers' slabs.

Along the Suffolk coast, it is possible to buy fish from the fishermen at the harbour towns of Aldeburgh and Southwold. The range on offer depends on the weather but is likely to include many flat fish, such as dab and plaice. Herrings are caught during the Autumn and Winter months and are smoked in Great Yarmouth, Norfolk. Known as 'red herrings', Yarmouth's very best are sold in THE FISH SHOP, England Lane, Gorleston, Great Yarmouth (Telephone 0493 732007).

Smoked fish is actually a thriving side-line for many of the fishing towns. Cley-next-the-Sea, where sprats, cod and haddock are landed is known for its smoked roes, a flavoursome delicacy available all over the country. For local smoked roes, however, Cley Smoke House (Telephone 0263 740282) is the place to visit.

Shellfish reign supreme; there are crabs from Cromer, mussels from Brancaster, shrimps from King's Lynn, lobsters from Sheringham and whelks from Wells-next-the-Sea. Colchester in Essex is famed for its oysters, in season whenever there is a letter 'r' in the month. As far as freshwater fish are concerned, eels swim into the estuaries from the warm Gulf Stream – and make a very popular dish throughout the region.

HOT BUTTERED CRAB

4 medium sized crabs
1 small clove garlic
2 anchovy fillets
4 oz/110 g/½ cup butter
2 fl oz/60 ml/4 tbs white wine
juice of 1 lemon
1 g/¼ tsp nutmeg
cayenne pepper, to taste
2 oz/60 g/4 tbs fresh white breadcrumbs
salt and pepper
parsley, chopped

Extract all the meat from the crabs, wash and reserve the shells. Finely chop garlic and anchovies and gently fry in a little butter for about 3 minutes. Add the wine, lemon juice and remainder of the butter, nutmeg and cayenne pepper. Stir in the breadcrumbs and crab meat, reserving enough breadcrumbs for the topping. Season to taste. Cook for approximately 5 minutes. Add chopped parsley. Transfer the buttered crab to the crab shells and cover each one with a little parsley and remaining breadcrumbs. Finish under the grill.

Serves 4 or may serve 8 if served on hot buttered toast as an appetiser or starter

SAMPHIRE

This marsh plant does grow in other regions but only in East Anglia is it so regularly harvested and appreciated. Generally it is served fresh as a vegetable but it can also be pickled in vinegar. It is quite salty so soak it in cold water first, rinse well and cook briefly in a large amount of boiling water. Serve with butter. It is delicious mixed with mussels, oysters or clams. Also try cooking in a little wine and cream with shallots.

CAISEY FISHERIES, 1 Oakwood Hill, Loughton, Essex
Telephone: 081 508 4372
Charlie Caisey, an active campaigner for traditional fishmongery, has sold fresh fish and shellfish from his shop in Loughton for more than 25 years. Despite being located away from the town's main thoroughfare, Caisey Fisheries continues to draw customers from all over Essex. They are attracted by the colourful display of fish which Charlie and his staff change every day and also by the very special type of service they know they will receive.

A busy market day in Sudbury, Suffolk

Most of Britain's vegetable crops are grown in the fertile fields of East Anglia, from potatoes and carrots to the more unusual vegetables like celeriac.

DENIS CURTIS'S CELERIAC AND CARROT SOUP

8 oz/225 g/1½ cups onion, sliced
2 leeks, cleaned and sliced
3 oz/85 g/¼ cup butter
2 lb/900 g/6 cups celeriac, peeled and sliced
1 lb/450 g/3 cups carrots, peeled and sliced
80 fl oz/2.4 litres/8 cups chicken stock
1 bouquet garni
2 bay leaves
4 g/1 tsp mild curry powder
10 ml/2 tsp balsamic vinegar
1 good handful of crushed praline
½ fl oz/15 ml/1 tbsp lemon juice
10 fl oz/290ml /1 cup double cream
nutmeg
salt and freshly ground pepper

Saute the onion and leeks in butter over a gentle heat until the onion softens. Add the celeriac and carrot. Cover with chicken stock and bring slowly to the boil and then simmer. Add bouquet garni, bay leaves and curry powder, first dissolved in balsamic vinegar, and praline. Simmer until the vegetables are tender, about 1 hour. Remove the bay leaves and bouquet garni. Liquidise. Push through a sieve into a clean pan. Add lemon juice and cream. Season lightly with salt and a good grinding of black pepper and a pinch of nutmeg.

Serves 12

EAST LINCOLNSHIRE GROWERS, London Road, Kirton, Boston
Telephone: 0205 722666
Based in Kirton, Lincolnshire, ELGRO is a marketing body set up 25 years ago to help its 46 farmer members promote their vegetables both in the UK and abroad. The group as a whole produces an enormous range of vegetables, including onions, potatoes, cauliflower, broccoli, spring greens, Brussels sprouts, white/green/red cabbage, leeks and celeriac.

Tender stalks of asparagus being gathered by hand

One of the lasting impressions as you travel through the countryside during June is field after field of bright yellow MUSTARD seed flowers. Two different types of seed are actually grown, brown and white, which are milled and then blended together.

The country's best-known mustard company, Colman's is based in Norwich. Colman's was originally established in 1823 and its distinctive yellow packaging has become familiar worldwide. In 1973, The Mustard Shop and Museum was opened in Bridewell Alley, Norwich, incorporating displays of historical production methods as well as the entire range of Colman's products.

THE MUSTARD SHOP is open all year round from 9.00 am to 5.30 pm every weekday except Tuesday, when it opens at 9.30 am. It is closed on Sunday. Telephone 0603 627889

Until the 16th century, ASPARAGUS grew wild throughout the region. It was commercially cultivated in the 17th century and by the beginning of the 19th century, England was the world's largest asparagus grower.

Asparagus has a very limited season – officially from 1st May, although warm weather may bring this forward into mid April, through to 21st June. Fresh asparagus should always be cooked very quickly, with the heads uppermost to stop them becoming soggy and falling off. 12 minutes in boiling water should be sufficient.

NORFOLK TURKEY BREAST WITH ASPARAGUS

4 portions skinned turkey breast
2 oz/56 g/2 tbs plain flour
½ oz/15 g/1 tbs butter
½ pt/290 ml/1 cup chicken stock
4 g/1 tsp fresh chopped sage
¼ pt/150 ml/¼ cup fresh cream
2 oz/56 g/½ cup cooked, diced ham
salt and freshly ground black pepper
8 oz/225 g/1¾ cup cooked asparagus stalks

Season turkey breasts and lightly coat with flour and fry in butter until lightly browned on both sides. Add chicken stock and sage. Cover and cook gently for 15–20 minutes or until tender. 5 minutes before end of cooking time, stir in the cream and the diced ham. Season to taste. To serve, arrange asparagus stalks over the turkey.

Serves 4

WHEAT and BARLEY are the most extensively farmed crops in East Anglia, combining with the relatively new rape-seed to fill the fields for miles. The land is perfect for wheat, in particular, with its good drainage, medium to heavy loam and alluvial soils.

Vivid yellow fields of flowering mustard

WORKING MILLS

DOWNFIELD WINDMILL, Fordham Road, Soham, Cambridgeshire
Telephone: 0353 720333

THE MILL, Over, Cambridgeshire
Telephone: 0954 30742

LETHERINGSETT WATERMILL, Riverside Road, Letheringsett, Holt, Norfolk
Telephone: 0263 713153
There has been a watermill, driven by the River Glaven, at Letheringsett for 900 years – it was even mentioned in the Domesday Book. The present watermill was built in 1802 and has been lovingly restored to all its former glory. All the original machinery is still in place and any maintenance work is carried out using traditional tools and working methods.

The mill uses solely East Anglian produced wheat to make 100% wholemeal stone-ground flour, currently around $2\frac{1}{2}$ tonnes per week. Plans are in hand to make the mill fully organic by accepting only organic wheat.

The watermill may be viewed all year round at the following times:
Tuesday to Friday from 9.00 am to 1.00 pm,
2.00 pm to 5.00 pm
Saturday from 9.00 am to 1.00 pm
Sunday from 2.00 pm to 5.00 pm,
Whitsun to September only
Demonstrations of traditional flour milling techniques may be seen every Tuesday, Thursday and Sunday from 2.00 pm to 4.00 pm.

A visit to an old working mill is a fascinating step back into the past

Windmills like this one at How Hill in Norfolk are still a familiar sight in East Anglia

It is surprising, when travelling around the eastern counties, how many PUBS suddenly appear seemingly out of nowhere, hidden behind a small outcropping of trees or in the middle of a tiny village. Many of these small country pubs are renowned for their excellent food, as well as for their beer, and faithful customers travel regularly out from the larger towns for Sunday lunch in their favourite one.

THE RATCATCHER'S INN, Cawston, Near Diss, Norfolk
Eugene Charlier's imagination and talent with locally grown ingredients was officially acknowledged in the summer of 1990, when the Ratcatchers' Inn won first prize in the Food from Britain Norfolk Pub Menu Competition.

Eugene prides himself on making use of Norfolk produce and has built up a good relationship with many local suppliers. He buys his hams from BROADLAND HAMS of Norwich (Telephone: 0603 412125) and his guinea fowl from ARK FOODS of Diss (Telephone: 0379 870717). His clientele come from as far as London to enjoy traditional Norfolk fare such as Sprowston sausage and home-made onion bread.

With such an abundance of locally milled flour and succulent soft fruits, it is no surprise to find that home baking is as strong a tradition as in the rest of the country. Grantham in Lincolnshire bakes its own special type of gingerbread, irresistibly chewy and full of spice. CATLIN BROS. at 11 High Street, Grantham (Telephone 0476 590345) not only sell home-baked gingerbread but also Lincolnshire dough cake and other local specialities.

The eastern counties, in particular Norfolk, have the culinary advantage of containing some of Britain's oldest and grandest country houses. Guests were, and still are, entertained during their stay by being taken out to shoot; although landowners avoid over-shooting through strict controls, East Anglian game has always been prolific.

RABBIT CASSEROLE WITH DUMPLINGS

Dumplings are a firm favourite in East Anglia and fresh wild rabbit is still a popular, economical choice in the region.

1 wild rabbit, jointed
6 oz/170 g/3 cups streaky bacon
2 large onions, sliced
8 oz/225 g/1¾ cups carrots, sliced
8 oz/225 g/1¾ cups mushrooms
1 apple, peeled, cored and diced
bouquet garni
2 oz/56 g/2 tbs flour
¼ pt/150 ml/½ cup white wine or dry cider
¾ pt/425 ml/1½ cups chicken stock
salt and pepper

DUMPLINGS

3 oz/85 g/¾ cup self raising flour
½ oz/15 g/1 tbs shredded beef suet
½ oz/15 g/1 tbs chopped fresh parsley or chives

Heat the oven to 170°C/325°F/Gas Mark 3. Roughly chop the bacon and fry gently in a flame-proof casserole with the rabbit pieces and onion until browned. Add the carrots, mushrooms, apples and bouquet garni and sprinkle over the flour. Stir to coat with flour. After a minute, pour in the wine and stock. Cover and bake in the oven for 1½ hours.

Meanwhile, make the dumplings by mixing the flour, suet, parsley or chives, salt and pepper together with just enough cold water to make a soft dough. Form the dumplings by rolling the mixture into 12 little balls. 30 minutes before the end of the cooking time, put the dumplings on top of the casserole, cover again and continue to bake until the rabbit is tender and the dumplings are cooked through.

Serves 4

FELBRIGG HALL, Felbrigg, Norwich
Telephone: 026375 444
Felbrigg is a beautiful 17th century house set in extensive parklands, surrounded by woods. Inside, exquisite 18th century furniture fills each room while the walled gardens contain traditional herbaceous borders, greenhouses, roses, fruit trees, vegetables, a herb border and an elegant dovecot.

The Hall and the gardens are open to the public from 30 March to 27 October on Monday, Wednesday, Thursday, Saturday and Sunday from 1.30 pm to 5.30 pm.

There is also a restaurant run by Joan Mapperley which serves local food cooked in a traditional kitchen with antique equipment. It is open throughout the year and is accessible from the park.

Long gone are the 18th century days when TURKEYS were driven on foot from Norfolk to the markets in London, a journey which could take up to 3 months. However, turkeys remain the most widely-bred bird in the region, their popularity extending far beyond the county borders.

There has been a return to more natural, less intensive rearing methods for turkeys, resulting in a growing taste for the fuller flavoured birds. There has also been a revival of interest in some of the older breeds, such as the large Norfolk Black and the Bronze Turkey.

SUFFOLK SMOCK COMPANY, Kyson Hill, Woodbridge, Suffolk
Telephone: 0394 383429
From an enthusiasm for rare breed pigs, Sarah Pinfold has developed the Suffolk Smock Company into one of the region's most successful specialist food producers.

Of particular note are Sarah's NORFOLK BLACKS, the big turkeys which were once so prolific in Norfolk and a breed which is again being revived. The Norfolk Black is the perfect Christmas turkey, so Sarah will be buying 250 poults in the Spring which will be allowed to roam free while feeding on berries and fruit, ready for the huge local festive demand.

Once again rivalling turkey in popularity as the Christmas bird, the GOOSE is now to be found roaming free on many farms. High in protein and at its best when non-intensively reared, the goose lives up to all the demands of the health-conscious as well as tasting deliciously rich.

NORFOLK GEESE, Chestnut Fram, Pulham Market, Diss, Norfolk
Telephone: 0379 676391
John Adlard is Chairman of the British Goose Producers' Association, a position for which he is eminently well qualified, having reared geese on Chestnut Farm for 15 years.

The birds spend most of their lives active outdoors, feeding on grass, only going into sheds when they are very young and unfeathered. There are currently 65,000 goslings on the farm, being fattened for Christmas.

John's brother, David Adlard, runs one of Britain's most highly acclaimed restaurants, the eponymously named Adlard's in Norwich. Poultry features on the menu, but fish and shellfish play a more major role, especially lobster and mussels.
ADLARD'S, Upper St. Giles Street, Norwich
Telephone: 0603 633522

After poultry, PIGS are the most widely farmed and valuable live-stock in the eastern counties. There are many popular pork products being produced in the region today which were originally eaten out of economy, pork being plentiful even in hard times. Huntingdon Fidget Pie also makes use of the abundance of apples in the region, while the range of hams and bacons on offer in many butcher's shops is unrivalled.

THE ESSEX PIG

Until the late 1960s, Essex had its own breed of pig, descended from small half-wild swine which used to be herded across the country in the Middle Ages. The original animals would forage for food around the Essex coast.

The Essex pig was highly prized for its pork and bacon; it lived and bred for up to 11 years, producing around 8 pigs per litter – fewer than many other breeds but the young animals were universally very strong and healthy.

In Dunmow, Essex, the bacon is so desirable that local married couples compete for a side, or flitch, of bacon each year. Known as the Dunmow Flitch Trial, each couple has to prove that they are happily married and the seemingly happiest are awarded the flitch.

BRYAN PICKERING, High Street, Old Costessey, Norwich
Telephone: 0603 742002
On January 19 1959, the Pickering family took over the village butcher's shop in Old Costessey, just outside Norwich in Norfolk. Few products were processed and supplies were received from local farms and then prepared in the shop itself. Although a wider range of tastes are now catered for, and the shop stocks a variety of continental hams and sausages, Bryan Pickering believes that many of the traditional, hand-made products will soon be his best-sellers again. Demand for sausages blended to his grandfather's Norfolk recipe, one of 46 different types, is enormous and he has noticed more orders coming in for chitterlings, pigs fry, pork cheese and ox liver – all popular back in 1959.

RED HOUSE FARM, North Scarle, Lincoln
Telephone: 052277 224
The Jones's produce a huge range of speciality products on their own premises about 10 miles outside Lincoln. In addition to superb Lincolnshire sausages, using prime local pork and herbs, Red House Farm also sells raised pork pies, potted beef and a local pork speciality called haslet.

Domestic APPLE growing continues to be hugely successful, especially as demand for old-fashioned and unusual varieties increases. Regular sunshine and rainfall make the region ideal for apple-growing; its rather exposed position, however, meant that severe damage was wreaked upon more than 600,000 apple trees in the storms which swept across much of South-Eastern England in 1987.

MOST POPULAR VARIETIES OF BRITISH APPLE

COX'S ORANGE PIPPIN: a firm, crisp and juicy apple which accounts for almost 60% of the dessert apple market.

CRISPIN: a medium-sized crisp apple which is best eaten chilled.

EGREMONT RUSSET: our most important russet apple which is becoming increasingly popular

ELSTAR: Voted 'Most Eatable Apple' in 1985.

GALA: crisp, sweet and juicy with a bright skin.

GLOSTER '89: available from late November to early March, it has creamy white flesh.

IDARED: Keeps for long periods of time – extremely juicy.

JONAGOLD: a large, striped apple voted 'Most Eatable Apple' in 1986.

KATY: developed in 1981, this crisp apple appears early in the season.

MALLING KENT: Another relatively new variety with orange, chewy skin.

SPARTAN: A colourful apple, turning from pale green to deep maroon as it ripens.

BRAMLEY'S SEEDLING: the most famous and most prolific cooking apple, with coarse, slightly acidic flesh.

OLIVERS ORCHARD, Olivers Lane, Gosbecks Road, Colchester, Essex
Telephone: 0206 331369
Olivers Orchard is not just an apple orchard. Vegetables and other types of fruit are also grown and are available on a Pick-Your-Own basis or from the farm shop. The range of apples is, however, what makes Olivers Orchard so interesting – some of the most unusual apples in Britain are grown here. The farm also produces and sells cider, fruit, juice and jams and visitors are more than welcome to wander round.

The dry, warm sun tempered by equally dry winds upon the rich peaty soil of the fields of inland East Anglia is perfect for many SOFT FRUITS. Essex, in particular, enjoys a soft-fruit industry so successful that many forms of diversification have been established, including jam making. Tiptree and Elsenham, two of England's most famous jam companies, are based in Essex.

Late British summer would not be complete without a Sunday spent picking bucketfuls of strawberries or blackberries, most of which are eaten on the way home. Those which survive are either eaten later for tea with fresh cream or made into delicious jams. When the labelled jars are opened in the cold winter months which follow, the smell of the fruit brings back all the summer memories.

Midsummer Pudding

MIDSUMMER PUDDING

7 slices white bread, crusts removed
6 oz/170 g/¾ cup blackcurrants
6 oz/170 g/¾ cup redcurrants
8 oz/225 g/1 cup raspberries
8 oz/225 g/1 cup strawberries
6 oz/170 g/¾ cup caster sugar, optional
mint leaves to decorate

Line a 3 pt/1.7 litre/6 cup pudding basin with the bread, keep some to cover the fruit. Remove the stalks from the fruit and wash. Place in a saucepan with 1 fl oz/30 ml/2 tbs of water and the sugar if you wish. Cook until the currants start to burst their skins, about 5 minutes. While the fruit is still warm, spoon into the lined basin and cover with the rest of the bread. Put a plate on top of the basin and press down with a weight or heavy pot. Place the pudding basin on a plate and leave overnight in the refrigerator. Reserve any juice that has been pressed out of the pudding and pour it into a small jug. Turn out the pudding onto a serving plate, pour over the reserved juice and decorate with mint leaves.

(MIDSUMMER HOUSE)

BELVOIR FRUIT FARM, Belvoir, Near Grantham, Lincolnshire
Telephone: 0476 870286
Belvoir Fruit Farm, growing a mouth-watering range of soft fruits including strawberries, raspberries, tayberries, red and black currants, gooseberries and blackberries, is open to the public every day during the summer months from 10.00 am to 8.00 pm. Much depends on the weather; if summer comes early, then fruit is ready for picking in late June. The season usually comes to a close towards the end of August, although blackberries will continue to flourish well into a warm Autumn.

Lord John Manners of Belvoir Castle makes old-fashioned fruit cordials from fruit picked on the estate. The cordials are sold all over the country and can also be bought from the house shop. The range on offer includes elderflower, strawberry, raspberry and blackcurrant.

Both the Romans and Normans are known to have acknowledged the good grape-growing potential of the eastern counties and the region now boasts around 300 acres of vines, yielding almost half a million bottles of WINE per year. As the British climate improves, so production increases and in good years, each acre of vineyard will produce up to 4000 bottles of fine wine.

VINEYARDS TO VISIT

CHILFORD ONE HUNDRED, Chilford Hall, Balsham Road, Linton, Cambridgeshire
Telephone: 0223 892641
7.4 hectares of vines.
Open in the summer only, tours available by appointment. Chilford Hall has its own winery but tastings will be charged for. There is also a shop and much to interest those keen on historical artefacts at Chilford. Refreshments can be organised if prior notice is given.

ELMHAM PARK, Elmham House, North Elmham, Dereham, Norfolk
Telephone: 036 281 571
1.4 hectares of vines.
The winery offers free tastings to visitors and there is also a picnic area.

BRUISYARD, The Winery, Church Road, Bruisyard, Saxmundham, Suffolk
Telephone: 072 875 281
4 hectares of vines.
Open in the summer only, tours available by appointment. Bruisyard also has its own winery with free tastings for visitors. Light refreshments are available from the restaurant and estate wine and other farm produce may be bought from the shop. Bruisyard also has magnificent gardens and a peaceful picnic area, making it suitable for children to visit, too.

WEST OF ENGLAND

THE Western-most part of England has held a certain fascination to visitors for centuries, with its irresistible combination of dramatic coastline and sheltered bays; its desolate moorlands and high-hedged country lanes; and its sedate towns and picturesque villages. A region of contrasts, it attracts more holidaymakers than any other part of the country.

The Severn estuary, flowing up from the Bristol Channel and through the Mendip Hills, leads to the elegant and sophisticated towns of Bath in Avon and Cheltenham in Gloucestershire where fine food and elegant Georgian architecture go hand in hand – and the long coastline also yields a wide variety of fish and shellfish, including many of the prime species much prized throughout the world, such as turbot, brill and Dover sole.

From the lush and sunny valleys of the Devon countryside comes rich dairy produce, like butter, cream and milk, as well as hams and bacons from the still thriving pig-breeding community. The orchards of Somerset and Dorset yield apples perfect not only for crunching but also for cider-making, a tradition which has developed way beyond its original purpose as a form of payment for farm labourers.

CLOTTED CREAM, surely one of the region's, if not Britain's, most celebrated products, is a direct result of the richness of local milk. Ideally, it should be made from butterfat from one herd only, fed on the same pasture. Guernsey and Jersey herds produce milk with a suitably high butterfat content of around 5.5%. When the milk is scalded over steam, the cream rises to the top and forms a thick, yellow crust as it cools.

Left: *The pretty Cornish fishing village of Polperro*
Right: *A welcoming invitation from Badgworthy in North Devon!*

Another popular and profitable form of diversification for dairy farmers is ice-cream making, which ties in particularly well with the seaside tourist trade. Jersey herds produce milk ideal for this purpose.

Few who visit the West Country can resist the ultimate temptation – the CREAM TEA. Scones (light and warm from the oven) or Cornish splits (much richer) are filled with clotted cream and topped with strawberry jam. All the ingredients can be found locally and combined, make one of the country's most delicious, if fattening, treats.

CHEDDAR

It is fitting that the country's richest dairying region should be responsible for one of the world's most famous cheeses, Cheddar. Originally produced in the 30 miles surrounding Wells Cathedral in Somerset, Cheddar cheese had become highly prized and subject to inferior imitation by the 18th century, when it was strictly defined as being made of the unpasteurised milk of a limited herd, in a recognisable cheese shape (ie. not a block) and properly matured – for up to 2 years. In 1939, there were over 500 recognised authentic Cheddar cheesemakers – by 1974, their number had been reduced to 32.

Today, as increased awareness of the qualities of traditional cheesemaking techniques combines with a wider knowledge of how the real thing should taste and look, makers of Farmhouse Cheddar are becoming increasingly widespread and successful.

A delicious Devonshire Cream Tea

COTEHALE HOUSE, St Dominick, Near Saltash, Cornwall
Telephone: 0579 50434
1,300 acre estate including a manor house, a watermill and a tea-shop on the quay – the perfect setting for the perfect cream tea.

Cream teas are not the sole domain of visitors to Cornwall. When in Somerset, compare and contrast by taking tea at:
HORNSBURY MILL, Near Chard
Telephone: 04606 3317
Hornsbury Mill dates back to around 1800, although there has been a mill on the site since 1327. As well as enjoying local produce in the restaurant, visitors can tour the grounds, including the trout lake, a museum of old kitchen and farm equipment, a small shop selling preserves and confectionery and five beautiful acres of gardens.

J B QUICKE & PARTNERS, Woodley, Newton St. Cyres, Devon
Telephone: 0392 851222   Contact: Tom Langdon-Davies
Quickes produce a wide range of traditional cheeses, including smoked and unsmoked Cheddar and Cheddar with herbs. They also produce ice cream and a range of bacons.

STREATFIELD HOOD & CO LTD., Denhay Farm, Broadoak, Bridport, Dorset
Telephone: 0308 22770/22717   Contact: Amanda Streatfield
Streatfield Hood are famous for their Farmhouse Cheddar, known as the Dorset Drum because of its distinctive shape. The drums are available from the farm and also from most specialist food shops in the UK.

BLUE VINNEY

This revival of interest in traditional cheese has also given rise to the re-emergence of Blue Vinney from Dorset, a blue-veined cheese made from the buttermilk of Old Gloucester cows. Disappearing from production during the Second World War, Blue Vinney was the subject of much rumour and speculation for years, with mysterious stories circulating of clandestine cheese-making in remote farmhouses. The mystery has now begun to clear, with Dorset farmer Mike Davies authentically producing one of the country's best loved cheeses.

Blue Vinney is available from Selfridges and Harrods in London, as well as from selected delicatessens in Dorset, Somerset and Yorkshire.

MIKE DAVIES, Woodbridge Farm, Stock Gaylard, Sturminster Newton, Dorset. Telephone: 0963 23216.
No sales from the farm.

BEENLEIGH BLUE

Beenleigh Blue is a cheese made from unpasteurised Friesian ewe's milk. Full-flavoured from 7 months of maturation, it is produced by farmer Robin Congdon and although still somewhat limited in supply, has gained international respect.

Available from the TICKLEMORE CHEESE SHOP, Ticklemore Street, Totnes, Devon. Telephone: 0803 865926.

DOUBLE & SINGLE GLOUCESTER

Cheesemaking in Gloucestershire was recorded as early as the 8th century, when wheels of local cheese were ceremonially rolled down the gentle hills of the Cotswolds, an odd custom which still exists today in Coopers Hill, between Gloucester and Cheltenham and in Randwick, near Stroud.

A fine collection of maturing Farmhouse Cheeses

It was not until after the end of the 16th century that Gloucester cheese was recognised beyond the Vales of Gloucester and Berkeley but soon it was being demanded by buyers across the country. The Gloucester cow, a large ancient breed, was responsible for the creaminess of the cheese's texture and for around 150 years, both cattle and cheese thrived.

In the mid 18th century, however, disease struck the breed and farmers introduced Longhorns and Shorthorns to make up the shortfall. Fifty years later, Gloucester cattle were almost extinct.

The difference between double and single Gloucester cheese has been disputed for years. Both cheeses have a diameter of approximately 39 cm; the single has a depth of 6 cm, while the double has a depth of 10.5 cm – so size is one factor. The milk used to make the cheese, whether it be from the morning yield or the evening yield, is also considered to be relevant.

GLOUCESTERSHIRE CHEESE AND ALE

From 'Good Things in England' by Florence White

1 oz/28 g/1 tbs English or Tewkesbury mustard
½ pt/290 ml/1 cup strong ale
6 oz/170 g/¾ cup Gloucester cheese, grated
4 slices toast

Heat the oven to 230°C/450°F/Gas Mark 8. Brush a deep casserole dish with the mustard. Pour in the ale and add the cheese. Bake in the oven for 15 minutes. Remove from oven and spoon melted cheese mixture over toast.

Serves 2

(THE LYGON ARMS HOTEL)

CHARLES MARTELL & SON, Laurel Farm, Dymock, Gloucestershire
In 1974, there were only 45 Gloucester cattle in Britain. Charles Martell formed the Gloucester Cattle Society, dedicated to reviving the much-loved breed and its cheese, and by 1979, the number of animals had risen to 100. Charles makes single Gloucester cheese from unpasteurised milk in 4 kg wheels, with no colourings. He also produces a double Gloucester and both cheeses may be bought at the markets in Cirencester, Gloucester and Ledbury.

Some of Britain's most prized FISH are caught off the coasts of Cornwall and Devon – sole, monkfish, John Dory, hake and skate – and those which are not whisked out of the region

instantly to London or beyond can be eaten fresh in local restaurants and hotels. The seas are rich in shellfish, from lobster, crab and scallops through to traditional sea-side fare like cockles, winkles, prawns and mussels.

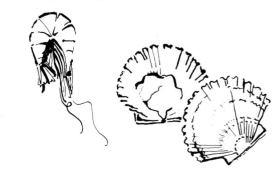

The dramatic, rocky Cornish coast line

FILLETS OF SOLE FROM PADSTOW

40 small mussels
3 fl oz/85 ml/⅓ cup dry cider
Dover sole fillets, about 3 oz/85 g each
2 oz/56 ml/¼ cup clotted cream
10 chives, cut into ¼ in/6 mm lengths, diagonally rather than
straight – they look better

Preheat the oven to 180°C/350°F/Gas Mark 4. Clean and wash the mussels in several changes of water. Place them in a saucepan with some of the cider over a high heat with the lid on, to open them. As soon as they have opened, empty them into a colander with a bowl underneath to collect the cooking juice. Remove the beards from all the mussels and discard the shells of all but 16.

Put the sole fillets in a shallow buttered dish and pour a little of the mussel cooking liquor over them. Cover with buttered paper and poach in the oven until just cooked through, about 5 minutes. Drain the poaching liquor into a small saucepan and add the remaining mussel liquor, the rest of the cider and the clotted cream. Bring to the boil and reduce by rapid boiling until the sauce coats the back of the spoon. Put the 24 shelled mussels, the 16 unshelled mussels and the chives in with the sauce and warm through. Put the fillets of sole on four warmed plates and pour the sauce and mussels over them.

(RICK STEIN AT THE SEAFOOD RESTAURANT, PADSTOW)

PILCHARDS, once fished in their millions between Harvest and Hallowe'en, have been replaced by MACKEREL in equal abundance; much of the local haul is, again, removed from the region, although some is kept and either sold fresh or sent to be smoked in one of the numerous smokehouses.

The three principal rivers running through the far west of the region, the Tamar, the Dart and the Exe, are home to SALMON and TROUT, while during May in Gloucestershire, the banks of the Severn are practically taken over by salmon fishing.

ELVERS have travelled from the shallow warm waters of the Atlantic up the Bristol Channel and down the Rhynes of Somerset ever since the region was half-submerged by water. They are caught in shoals in the marshy areas around Wells Cathedral and ELVER CAKE is still a great delicacy in Bath.

Probably the best way to experience the flavour of the south-west is to visit one of the many fishmongers and take your pick from the array of freshly caught fish and shellfish.

W HARVEY & SONS, Newlyn, Penzance, Cornwall
Telephone: 0736 62734
Cornish crabs freshly boiled and hand-picked crab meat.

SYLVESTER'S SEAFOODS, 2 Holt Cottages, Richmond Road, Appledore, near Bideford, Devon
Telephone: 0237 479101
A huge range of fish fresh from the sea. Cod and plaice are complemented by a variety of prime species, such as bass and Dover sole. Half a mile away, at Appledore Quay, you can see the fish actually being landed.

G & K SANDERS, 39 High Street, Budleigh Salterton, Devon
Telephone: 03954 3125
A very wide range of local prime fish, including John Dory, wrasse and the finest salmon from the River Tamar.

THE FISH & GAME STALL, The Market Hall, Torquay, Devon
Open Monday to Saturday from 8.00 am to 6.00 pm.
It is best to get to the market as early as possible to choose from the widest range of fresh fish and shellfish, including John Dory, bream and sea bass. There is also lots of locally smoked fish.

RICK STEIN'S FISH SOUP

2–3 lb/900 g–1.35 kg fish (conger eel, skate, huss, shark, any
mixed fish except oily ones)
3 pts/1.7 litres/6 cups water
5 fl oz/150 ml/½ cup olive oil
6 oz/170 g/1 cup onion, peeled and roughly chopped
6 oz/170 g/1 cup celery, washed and roughly chopped
6 oz/170 g/1 cup leek, washed and roughly chopped
6 oz/170 g/1 cup Florence fennel, roughly chopped
5 cloves garlic
2 in/5 cm piece of orange peel
10 oz/285 g tomatoes
10 ml/2 tsp tomato puree
¼ large red pepper, blistered under the grill and peeled
1 bayleaf
large pinch of saffron
salt and ground black pepper
large pinch of cayenne pepper

Fillet all the fish and use the heads and bones to make a fish
stock with the 3 pts/1.7 litres/6 cups of water. Heat the olive
oil in a large pan and add the onion, celery, leek, Florence
fennel and garlic. Cook until the vegetables are very soft –
about 45 minutes. Add the orange peel, tomatoes, tomato
puree, red pepper, bayleaf, saffron, and fish fillets. Cook
briskly, stirring constantly. Add the fish stock, bring to the
boil and simmer for 40 minutes. Liquidize the soup and pass
it through a conical strainer, pushing as much as you can
through with the back of a ladle. Return soup to pan and heat
gently. Season with salt, pepper and cayenne. The soup
should be a little on the salty side, with a subtle but
noticeable heat from the cayenne. Serve the soup with some
French bread (thinly sliced and fried in olive oil, then rubbed
with garlic), a bowl of grated cheese (Emmenthal or
Parmesan) and some rouille. Spread the croutons with rouille
and float them on the soup scattered with cheese.

Serves 4

(THE SEAFOOD RESTAURANT, PADSTOW)

Rouille is a thick sauce made from red chillies, garlic, olive oil
and tomato puree and is available ready-made from
delicatessens.

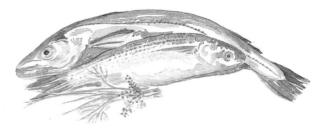

Fresh from the sea in Newlyn's fish market

There was a time when every West Country family owned a pig.
The meat would be treated in a method characteristic to the
region, so regional cures were established, again using ingredients peculiar to the locality. Every part of the pig was eaten and
the animal was fed and looked after in a way to ensure that this
was possible. Devon farmers became expert in breeding pigs
with precisely the right proportion of fat to lean, in order to
make local specialities such as hog or white pudding and
blended sausages.

Typical of West Country imagination in using all parts of the
animal is the BATH CHAP. The cut is taken from the jaw of fruit-fed
pigs, ideally retaining part of the jawbone and all of the tongue.
The small joints are then cured and, when required, eaten hot
with parsley sauce.

In Wiltshire in particular, cures were developed not only as a
method of preserving meat, but also to suit the tastes of the
county's inhabitants, using local honey and imported spices.
This led to a milder, sweeter, more palatable cure than in other

regions. Again, these cures are becoming popular again, offering a welcome contrast to the salty, bland taste so prevalent in mass-produced bacon and hams.

SOMERSET PORK

4 large boneless pork slices
2 oz/56 g/2 tbs seasoned plain flour
15–30ml/1–2 tbs oil
6 oz/175 g/¾ cup button mushrooms, cleaned and trimmed
½ pt/300 ml/1 cup dry cider
generous dash of Worcestershire sauce
salt and black pepper
2 oz/50 g/½ cup seedless raisins
15 ml/1 tbs lemon juice
4 fl oz/100 ml/½ cup single cream
freshly chopped parsley, to garnish

Trim the pork, if necessary, and coat well in half the seasoned flour. Fry in heated oil for 10 minutes, or until browned on both sides. Remove from pan and keep warm. Add the mushrooms to the pan and cook gently for 2–3 minutes, then stir in 1 tbs of the remaining seasoned flour and cook for about one minute. Gradually add the cider, stirring all the time, and bring to the boil. Add the Worcestershire sauce, plenty of seasonings, raisins and lemon juice and replace the pork. Cover and simmer for about 10 minutes until tender. Stir in the cream, adjust the seasonings and serve sprinkled with chopped parsley. Serve with boiled rice or pasta and a mixed green salad.

Serves 4

The world famous Cornish Pasty

HEAL FARM, Kingsnympton, Umberleigh, Devon
Telephone: 07695 2077
Contact Anne Petch to make an appointment to visit

Anne Petch has been rearing rare breed pigs in Devon for around 20 years; not only was Anne dismayed at the quantity of unnecessary additions she saw being included in animal feed on local farms but she also felt deeply about the ways in which animals were being kept.

She was therefore determined not to be involved in intensive farming methods but was equally determined to make a commercial success of her business. An enthusiastic campaigner for The Rare Breeds Survival Trust, she has integrated many old-fashioned types of pig into her stock. The benefits go way beyond the excellent flavour of the meat they produce – many breeds which would otherwise disappear are conserved.

"I do believe that great change is on the way in the farming world," says Anne. "As the countryside gets taken over for leisure activities, we will have to turn to the sturdy old breeds which can survive the less sheltered farmlands around the coast."

As for the end product, local success has developed into national acclaim. Each cut, trimmed to order, is free of any unnecessary additives and is full of the flavour that long maturation engenders. Heal Farm have diversified into hams, sausages and bacon and, in the near future, hope to branch out into wild boar, park-reared venison and high quality prepared dishes.

Perhaps Cornwall's most famous product, the CORNISH PASTY, has suffered widespread travesty over the years. The original pasty was designed as a convenient lunch for miners, a pastry case containing a meat-based filling at one end and a sweetened filling at the other, divided by a crimped wall. The intended eater's initials were often etched on the corner. The pasty spread, its recipe going wherever Cornish tin miners went to find work and developing on the way. Fillings were originally quite elaborate, based around meat, potato and onion, although leaner days led to sparser ingredients. There are still authentic Cornish pasties to be found, however, full of chunks of meat, rather than minced meat, and seasonal vegetables.

GINSTERS CORNISH PASTIES LTD., Tavistock Road, Callington, Cornwall
Telephone: 0579 83993
It did not take Ginsters long to discover that their traditional hand-made Cornish pasties were popular way beyond the region. From a small family business established in the late 1960s, Ginsters has grown to become a national operation supplying Cornish pasties all over the UK. Tradition is still very important, however and although Ginsters pasties are no longer all made by hand, quality and authenticity still reign supreme.

Georgian splendour in The Pump Room, Bath at tea-time

BATH has been enormously popular with tourists ever since the Romans built the city on the site of the only hot springs in Britain. The complex system of baths, designed to heal and to relax, attracted the wealthy from London who, for their part, brought a civilised and sophisticated attitude to food and eating.

PRIORY HOTEL, Weston Road, Bath
Telephone: 0225 331922
For a quintessentially English weekend, the Priory Hotel just outside the main town is hard to beat. Originally built in 1835 as a country residence, the hotel boasts many fine pieces of antique furniture and paintings as well as an excellent restaurant. There is also a croquet lawn, surrounded by beautiful countryside.

For food lovers, Bath itself has much to offer, from bakeries and cafes to well-known restaurants. At tea-time, try visiting the GEORGIAN PUMP ROOM where one can sample the famous Bath Bun – a light, sweet bun recorded as popular in Bath for at least two centuries. Bath Buns can also be bought from COBB'S in Westgate, a bakery established in 1866 which makes Bath Buns to an original 1679 recipe.

Also worth seeking out is SALLY LUNN'S HOUSE, 4 North Parade Passage, the oldest house in Bath. Housing a traditional kitchen bakery, this is the place where another of Bath's specialities, the Sally Lunn Bun, was supposedly created. A rich brioche-style bun which can be eaten as either a savoury or sweet snack, its nomenclature is debated – was it named after the girl who originally sold them in the street? Or is 'Sally Lunn' a badly-pronounced street-cry derived from the French 'soleil et lune'?

SHELDON MANOR

About 11 miles north-east of Bath stands Sheldon Manor, one of the region's most welcoming and interesting historic houses. Built circa 1282, Sheldon Manor has been home to the Gibbs family for 700 years; for the architects, there is the 13th century porch and 15th century chapel to fascinate, while gardeners may marvel at the terraced gardens and wide variety of roses.

The Gibbs are proud not only of their family home, but they are also eager to show visitors the variety and quality of locally grown and produced food available in the area. A summer buffet at Sheldon Manor might include home-cooked hams, local Chewton Cheddar cheese and a range of traditional chutneys and preserves. For dinner, served in the panelled dining room, there might be Lady Fettiplace's Rich Almond Soup made to a 16th century recipe followed by the Gibbs' own Roast Jacob lamb.

Many of the ingredients used at Sheldon Manor are provided by the local food producers' association, the Wiltshire Larder.

To arrange a visit, telephone Major or Mrs Gibbs on (0249) 653120.

When it comes to FRUIT, the West Country is undoubtedly famed for its apples. The range of English apples being grown at present is almost as wide as it was years ago. Their uses are also wide, from eating to cooking to cider-making to apple-wine-making to pig-feeding.

The mild climate also means that the region has a wealth of soft fruits to harvest, often through Pick-Your-Own ventures. Strawberries, blackberries, gooseberries, plums and apricots are all ripened naturally by the sun and available earlier than in any other part of the country.

Pick-Your-Own Farms are now popular places for weekend family outings

WHERE TO PICK YOUR OWN

BRYMPTON D'EVERCY, Estate Office, Yeovil, Somerset
Telephone: 0935 862528 – soft fruit

ELWELL FRUIT FARM, Netherbury, Bridport, Dorset
Telephone: 030888 283 – soft fruit

MCGUFFIE PARTNERSHIP, Thatch Cottage, Woolstone,
Bishopscleeve, Cheltenham, Gloucestershire
Telephone: 0242 673278 – apples, pears, plums

NORTH DEVON FARM PARK, Marsh Farm, Landkey, Barnstaple,
Devon
Telephone: 0271 830255 – soft fruit
North Devon Farm Park also includes 49 different breeds of
British sheep, a fish farm and Pick Your Own vegetable fields.

QUINCE OR DAMSON CHEESE

1 lb/450 g/2 cups fruit pulp, damson or quince
1 lb/450 g/2¼ sugar
fresh clotted cream

If using quince, halve the fruit, leaving the peel on and core
in. Leave the damsons whole. Stew them until they are
completely tender, then pass them very carefully through a
sieve leaving all the rough behind. When stewing the fruit,
use as little water as possible, just sufficient to stop the fruit
sticking to the pan. To every 1 lb of pulp, add 1 lb of sugar.
Boil fast, stirring all the time, until the mixture thickens. Pour
into flat rather than deep pots. Put the pots of damson cheese
in a warm place to dry out – in the past they used to be
placed in the airing cupboard for several days to assure a
luscious finished product. Serve as a sweetmeat at the end of
a meal, with Jersey cream.

(SHELDON MANOR)

CIDER

Cidermakers rarely begin as cidermakers – it is often a successful
sideline which eventually becomes the orchard's main
business. It is a very time-consuming business, too, and one
which depends heavily upon plenty of sunshine, regular rainfall
and impeccable storage conditions.

Originally, cider was made for the farmer's family and for the
farm's labourers. A tart taste is preferred, made from apples high
in acid and tannin. Farms which continue to make cider in the
traditional way – apples are pulped and pressed and the juice
run off into barrels to ferment naturally – produce 'scrumpy',
refreshing, tart and very potent. It is particularly popular with
cider aficionados.

THE ORIGINAL CORNISH SCRUMPY COMPANY, Callestock
Cider Farm, Penhallow, Truro, Cornwall
Telephone: 0872 573356
See for yourself how five acres of apple orchards become bottles
of traditional farmhouse cider. Every stage of the process can be
viewed from the farm, including pressing, fermenting and
bottling to provide an insight into the way cider-making has
developed over the years. The finished product may also be
purchased.

The warm and moist south-facing slopes of inland West Country
are ideal for growing GRAPES. Devon and Somerset, in particular,
are rich in viticulture and have several highly acclaimed wines
to their name. Most vineyards are happy to receive visitors
given advance notice.

LODDISWELL, Lilwell, Loddiswell, Kingsbridge, Devon
Telephone: 0548 550221
2.4 hectares of vines.
Open in the summer only, guided tours available by
appointment.
Free wine tastings are offered to visitors and bottled wine is
available from the shop. Light refreshments can also be arranged
but must be booked in advance. Children are also welcome at
Loddiswell – there is a special play area for them.

SHARPHAM, Sharpham House, Ashprington, Totnes, Devon
Telephone: 080 423 203
3 hectares of vines.
Open in the summer only, guided tours available by
appointment.
The vineyard has its own winery and free tastings for visitors, as
well as a shop selling estate wines and other farm produce.

THREE CHOIRS, Rhyle House, Welsh House Lane, Newent,
Gloucestershire
Telephone: 053 185 225/555
14.5 hectares of vines.
Open all year round, guided tours available by appointment.
Three Choirs is a large vineyard with its own winery and shop, as
well as free tastings for visitors. Set in lovely countryside, there is
also a picnic area.

AVALON, East Pennard, Shepton Mallet, Somerset
Telephone: 074986 393
1.42 hectares of organically-managed vines.
Open in the summer only, guided tours available by
appointment.
There is also a shop selling estate wines and other farm produce.

PILTON MANOR, Pilton, Shepton Mallet, Somerset
Telephone: 074989 325
9 hectares of vines.
Open in the summer only, guided tours available by
appointment.
Pilton Manor has its own winery offering free tastings to visitors,
as well as a shop and a small restaurant serving light refreshments.

LONDON AND SOUTH-EAST ENGLAND

Few cities can boast such a wide variety of food shops as London. The foodhalls of Harrods, Selfridge's and Fortnum and Mason are huge and elaborate, selling the best of Britain's fresh and prepared foods. But there are also cheese factors, fish shops, bread shops, specialist fruit and vegetable shops and the most amazing international delicatessens to be found.

Immigration has given valuable variety to London's food and drink, to the point where delicacies from almost every part of the world are accessible in the capital today. Markets specialising in Chinese, Indian and Mediterranean food thrive in the city, and the main markets can choose from a wider range of imported produce to complement domestic supplies.

As a consequence, the people of London and the South-East have perhaps developed more experimental tastebuds than those in the Northern and Western regions. Distribution further than the south-east was almost impossible until relatively recently, so the exotic produce landed along the south coast and the Port of London remained the domain of the locals.

HARRODS, Knightsbridge, London SW1
Telephone: 071 730 1234

SELFRIDGE'S, 400 Oxford Street, London W1
Telephone: 071 629 1234

FORTNUM & MASON, Piccadilly, London W1
Telephone: 071 734 8040

NEAL'S YARD, 9 Neal's Yard, London WC2
Telephone: 071 379 7646

HOBBS OF MAYFAIR, 29 South Audley Street, London W1
Telephone: 071 409 1058

The gently meandering River Thames at Abingdon

EUROTECA, 359 Fulham Road, London SW10
Telephone: 071 351 7825
One of London's newest and finest specialist food shops, Euroteca combines the best of everything – a butcher who produces his own sausages, a fishmonger whose species extends from the traditional to the exotic, a baker who makes breads from all over the world and an extraordinary selection of delicatessen goods. Locals can also pop in for a bite at lunchtime; soups, pies, stews and enormous sandwiches are made fresh every day.

London has three main markets, all of which are international trading centres for the world's finest produce. Steeped in history and retaining much of their original customs and regulations, they are a strange mixture of friendly bantering and closed-shop insularity.

Neal's Yard Dairy in Covent Garden carries a dazzling array of the finest British Cheeses

- BILLINGSGATE MARKET, West India Dock Road, London E14
  Superintendent: Mr David Butcher
  Telephone: 071 987 1118
Gone are the days when small vessels unloaded fish from the Thames into the majestic arches of the old market in Upper Thames Street. Chartered by Edward I in 1272 and under the control of the Corporation of London since the 17th century, Billingsgate was moved to new premises in London's developing dockland area in 1982. Most fish now arrives by air and refrigerated lorry, from all over the world. Despite the march of progress upon the fish market, ancient customs, such as the handing down of stalls from generation to generation and the complex grading of the various porters, still exist.

- NEW COVENT GARDEN MARKET, Nine Elms, London SW8
  Superintendent's Office Telephone: 071 720 4465
England's largest wholesale fruit, vegetable and flower market moved from its original site in Covent Garden in 1974 in order to accommodate its rapid development. The present market is more or less divided into two, one half trading in fruit and vegetables and the other in flowers and plants. Everyday staples like potatoes, carrots, apples and pears lie next to imported exotica like okra, squash, kiwi fruit and mangos. It is a truly international market, attracting buyers from all over the world.

- SMITHFIELD MARKET, Smithfield, London EC2
  Superintendent: Mr Douglas Noakes
  Telephone: 071 236 8734
A cattle market was established by the Corporation of London on a site known as Smithfield in 1638. Slaughtering and sales of live animals were eventually outlawed in the market, leaving the sales of carcasses, cuts and game which exist today.

As well as the large international markets, there is a proliferation of smaller, much more accessible street markets where produce from all over the world can be bought. The range on offer will vary according to local demand. Berwick Street market in Soho therefore does a brisk trade in fresh green vegetables and oriental specialities, while the stalls of Brixton market overflow with colourful exotic fruit.

During the 19th century, London's population increased enormously and there were many mouths to be fed. Water supplies were very poor, time was more limited and overall standards of living remained low, so most meals were bought from street vendors and taverns.

The taverns served meals at a set time and at a set price, known as an 'ordinary'. Dishes and prices varied from tavern to tavern, with the more fashionable establishments gaining a reputation for particular dishes. YE OLDE CHESHIRE CHEESE (145 Fleet Street, London EC4A 2BU Telephone: 071 353 6170) became renowned for its huge savoury puddings, baked every Wednesday and Saturday during the winter. Little has changed at Ye Olde Cheshire Cheese – the beefsteak puddings are as

delicious as ever, despite the modern omission of oysters and larks. Beer or ale was the favourite tavern food accompaniment – and the British 'pint' is still as much in demand today.

> Also worth a visit is THE QUALITY CHOP HOUSE, 94 Farringdon Road, London EC1 (Telephone: 071 837 5093). Established in 1869, its present menu and decor have remained faithful to its origins. You can feast on calf's liver, veal sausages, fish cakes or steak, all served with mashed potato, fresh vegetables and gravy. The formula is simple – excellent ingredients and minimum fuss.

Historically, Londoners have also had a wide variety of take-away foods from which to choose, including hot eels and pea soup in the winter and hot eels with pickled whelks in the summer. The 19th century also saw the rise of the baked potato, served with salt and butter, often eaten as a meal in itself. Cold fried flounders, boiled sheep trotters, hot peas in clothbound tins, savoury pies and gingerbread were all sold in the city.

POTTED EEL AND MUSSELS
IN PARSLEY JELLY

14 oz/400 g fresh eel fillet, skinned
2 lb 3 oz/1 kg fresh mussels
3 hard-boiled eggs
2 lemons, peeled, pith removed, cut into small cubes
1 oz/28 g/4 tbs freshly chopped parsley
2 shallots, finely chopped
13 fl oz/375 ml/1½ cups dry white wine
9 fl oz/250 ml/1 cup fish stock
6 firm tomatoes, peeled, seeded, cut into small dice
salt and pepper, to taste

FOR JELLY

1¾ pts/1 litre/3½ cups fish stock, cold
2½ oz/70 g/½ cup onion, finely chopped
2½ oz/70 g/½ cup leak, finely chopped
2½ oz/70 g/½ cup tomato, finely chopped
8 oz/225 g chicken breast, minced
1 oz/28 g/2 tbs fresh tarragon
1 oz/28 g/2 tbs fresh parsley
1 oz/30 g powdered gelatine
2 egg whites
salt and pepper, to taste

To prepare the jelly, place all the vegetables and the herbs into a pan with the minced chicken breast. Season with salt and pepper. Add the two egg whites and beat together until the mixture is well amalgamated. Pour on the cold fish stock, bring slowly to the boil, stirring occasionally with a wooden spoon and allow to simmer gently for 20 minutes. Line a conical strainer with moist fine muslin cloth. Slowly pour the jelly through into a clean bowl. Allow to cool.

Now start the terrine. Cut the eel fillets into 4–5 in/12.5cm lengths. Place them in a poaching vessel with 9 fl oz/250 ml/1 cup of the white wine, the fish stock, 1 oz/28 g/2 tbs of the parsley, salt and pepper. Leave to marinate for one hour. Peel the hard boiled eggs, separate the whites and yolks, chopping them separately. Poach the eels in the marinade until cooked. Remove from the heat and drain the fillets on a clean cloth.

Place the washed mussels in a pan and pour on the remaining white wine. Cover with a tight fitting lid and steam for 2–3 minutes or until the shells are open, then drain. Remove the mussels from their shells. Remove any debris or beards within the mussels and allow to cool.

Pour a ladleful of the jelly into the bottom of a terrine, sprinkle with white of egg, yolk, diced tomato, lemon cubes, shallot, and chopped parsley. Lay some of the poached eel strips lengthways on top and some of the mussels Place in the refrigerator to set. Repeat the process until all the fish and garnish ingredients are used and the terrine is filled Chill for 24 hours.

To serve, turn the terrine out from its mould, having first dipped it into hot water for a few seconds. Cut into ½ in/1¾ cm slices. Serve the terrine with a watercress sauce, made by stirring a fine watercress puree into a basic mayonnaise sauce.

Serves 10–12

(PAUL GAYLER AT THE LANESBOROUGH HOTEL)

Take-away food shops are enjoying a minor renaissance in the capital at the moment, with many excellent fish and chip and pie and mash shops making sure that good value can also mean good quality. For wonderful fish and chips, try SEA SHELL FISH RESTAURANT AND TAKE-AWAY, 49 Lisson Grove, London NW1 (Telephone: 071 723 8703) or GEALES, 2 Farmer Street, London W8 7SN (Telephone: 071 727 7969). And for pie and mash, try F. COOKE & SONS, 41 Kingsland High Street, London E8 (Telephone: 071 254 6458) or GODDARD'S, 203 Deptford High Street, London SE8 (Telephone: 081 692 3601).

London was over a century behind Paris in the establishment of a restaurant trade. Across the Channel, a heated legal battle had been fought between cook-shop owners and shop-keeper M. Boulanger, when he introduced a range of soups and light snacks in his shop in 1765. M. Boulanger won the case and became the world's first restaurateur. In London, the taverns and the street vendors continued to enjoy a culinary monopoly until 1873, when London's first restaurant opened.

Thereafter, French chefs infiltrated London's gentlemen's clubs and grand hotels, culminating in Escoffier's introduction of the à la carte menu at the Carlton Hotel in 1899.

London's reputation as a centre of fine cooking and food was gradually established. At first, it tended to be foreign chefs who shone in Britain, attracted by the wide range of excellent ingredients. But British cooks soon began to develop their own sense of pride in their country's produce and recipes, adapting regional specialities for sophisticated London palates.

It is still easy to find many traditional London dishes in the capital. Steak, kidney and oyster pudding, roast beef, shank of lamb, any number of game dishes and a wide variety of comforting puddings are regularly served in restaurants like Simpsons, as well as in smaller, less well-known establishments.

QUAILS' EGGS WITH HADDOCK
AND CHEESE SAUCE

12 quails' eggs
1 lb/450 g smoked haddock
½ pt/290 ml/1 cup bechamel sauce
4 oz/110 g/½ cup grated cheese

Boil the quails' eggs for 2 minutes and peel. Steam the haddock, remove any skin and bone then flake the fish into a bowl. Make bechamel by melting 1½ oz/45 g/¼ cup butter in a pan then adding 1½ oz/45 g/¼ cup flour, stir and cook for a few minutes. Gradually stir in half a pint of milk to make a smooth sauce, season to taste. Stir a little of the sauce into the fish and divide between four dishes. Arrange three eggs in each dish and top with remaining sauce. Sprinkle the grated cheese over the sauce and brown under the grill.

Serves 4

(SIMPSONS RESTAURANT)

ANTON MOSIMANN'S BREAD
AND BUTTER PUDDING

'Dating from the early eighteenth century, this is an English nursery dish transformed. It has also become one of the best known recipes! It's an ideal pudding to serve at a Sunday lunch – but I also serve it at dinner parties, and it's always rather well received.'

18 fl oz/514 ml/1¾ cups milk
18 fl oz/514 ml/1¾ cups double cream
1 vanilla pod, split
a little salt
1½ oz/42 g/1½ tbs butter, melted
6 large eggs
9 oz/255 g/1 cup vanilla sugar
6 small soft bread rolls
1 oz/28 g/1 tbs sultanas, soaked in water and drained
4 oz/110 g/½ cup apricot glaze, warm
icing sugar

Heat the oven to 170°C/325°F/Gas Mark 3. Place the milk, double cream, salt, and vanilla pod into a pan and bring to the boil. Use a little of the butter to grease a large oval pie dish. Beat together the eggs and vanilla sugar until pale, then gradually add the milk and cream mixture, stirring. Cut the bread rolls into slices and butter them. Arrange in the base of the dish. Sprinkle over the sultanas. Pour in the milk mixture through a sieve. The bread will float to the top. Place the dish in a bain-marie on top of folded newspaper, and pour in hot water to come half way up the sides of the dish.

Poach carefully in the oven for 45–50 minutes. When the pudding is ready, it should wobble very slightly in the middle. Remove from the oven and cool a little. Brush a thin coating of glaze over the top of the pudding – either lump-free apricot glaze or sieved apricot jam, boiled with a little water until it falls in slow, sticky drops from the spoon. Just before serving, dust with icing sugar. Serve warm.

Serves 10

(MOSIMANN'S)

SIMPSONS-IN-THE-STRAND, 100 Strand, London WC2R 0EW
Telephone: 071 836 9112

THE GRENADIER, 18 Wilton Row, London SW1X 7NR
Telephone: 071 235 3074

RULES, 35 Maiden Lane, London WC2E 7LS
Telephone: 071 836 5314/2559

THE RITZ, Piccadilly, London W1V 9DG
Telephone: 071 493 8181

THE SAVOY GRILL, Strand, London WC2R 0EU
Telephone: 071 836 4343

THE ENGLISH GARDEN, 10 Lincoln Street, London SW3 2TS
Telephone: 071 584 7272

THE NEW SERPENTINE RESTAURANT, Hyde Park, London W2 2UH
Telephone: 071 402 1142

As well as a strong sense of tradition, London also boasts a wealth of innovative and creative chefs. Using the old British formula of top quality ingredients and simple cooking methods, chefs not only from Britain but all over the world are making their mark with their own interpretations of British dishes.

GARY RHODES at THE GREENHOUSE, 27a Hay's Mews, London W1X 7RJ
Telephone: 071 499 3331

ROWLEY LEIGH at KENSINGTON PLACE, 201 Kensington Church Street, London W8 7XL
Telephone: 071 727 3184

ANTHONY WORRALL THOMPSON at ONE-NINETY, 190 Queen's Gate, London SW7
Telephone: 071 581 5666

The fertile soil, the warm climate and the proximity of London have always ensured that south-eastern larders are well stocked.

Many of the rural South-East's farming traditions have disappeared in recent years but new activities such as vineyards as well as goat and sheep cheesemakers, have grown up in their place, all designed to delight south-eastern palates.

There are smart and expensive restaurants, country house hotels, seaside cafes and cosy tea shops – it is never difficult to find somewhere good to eat in the south-east.

THE MOCK TURTLE, 4 Pool Valley, Brighton, East Sussex
Telephone: 0273 27380
A traditional English tea shop in the heart of cosmopolitan Brighton, The Mock Turtle serves home-baked breads, cakes, pastries and buns with its tea and coffee – it's the sort of place you never want to leave.

The Thames flows through the verdant valleys and the prosperous towns of the Home Counties alike, and for centuries, members of the aristocracy have built palaces and mansions on its banks so that the borders of the city have gradually expanded, with once rural Chiswick, Richmond and Kew now considered part of London itself.

The original inhabitants of the south-eastern counties often had plenty of leisure time, resulting in many important sporting events being based in the region. Traditional country pursuits such as hunting, fishing and shooting remain popular in these outposts, and what you eat and drink at these social events is as important as who you are and what you wear. Seen at every sporting event of the season and one of the most refreshing drinks in the world, Pimm's has remained firmly southern-based. Its recipe is still a secret, as it was when shellfish merchant James Pimm sold the gin-based spirit in his oyster tavern in the City.

The river banks at Richmond provide an ideal setting for a picnic

To make the perfect Pimm's

Add two or three measures of lemonade to one measure of Pimm's No. 1 cup. Add plenty of ice, a slice of cucumber peel, a slice of lemon and a sprig of mint. Fresh fruit, such as strawberries and additional herbs, such as borage, may be added if desired.

The South-Eastern portion of England, stretching from the rich pasturelands of Hampshire up the south-facing slopes of Berkshire and then east into the warm and fertile lands of Kent, contains some of the country's most valuable and varied agricultural activity.

SKIRT OF BEEF
WITH ANCHOVY SAUCE

2 lb/900 g skirt of beef
4 oz/110 g/½ cup butter
2 oz/56 g/¼ cup shallots, chopped
4 fl oz/100 ml/½ cup dry white wine
1 bunch fresh tarragon, chopped
1 oz/28 g/1 tbs anchovy fillet
1 clove of garlic, peeled and blanched
¼ oz/1 g/2 tsp mustard powder
lemon juice
Worcestershire sauce
cognac

FOR MARINADE

peanut oil
olive oil
red wine

Mix together equal quantities of peanut oil, olive oil and red wine, sufficient to cover the meat. Marinate the skirt of beef for 24 hours.

Melt the butter, add shallots and cook gently, not allowing them to colour. Add white wine, tarragon and simmer for 5 minutes. Add the rest of the ingredients and cook for 10 minutes. Liquidise until smooth. Pour into a jug and keep warm.

Remove the skirt of beef from the marinade and trim off any fat or tendons. They will come away much more easily once the meat has been marinated. Dry the beef on kitchen paper and grill. Serve the meat medium rare with the sauce and garnish with fresh watercress.

Serves 4

(COLIN BUTTON AT THE HAMPSHIRE HOTEL)

Romney Marsh sheep are widely bred on the Kent and Sussex coast, feeding on the salty pastures. Strong winds from the Channel sweep across the marshes but these sheep are hardy enough to withstand them.

Lambing in the South-East begins in early Spring, with the best lamb being available between August and November. This then gives the young lambs time to feed on the summer pastures which adds so much flavour to their meat.

Food traditions are held in great esteem, with the Gressingham and Aylesbury duck being fiercely protected from imitation and revered English puddings such as Richmond Maids of Honour and Kentish huffkins still retaining their original names.

Kent is often referred to as 'The Garden of England', providing, as it has since the 16th century, a large proportion of the country's favourite fruit, in particular apples, pears, cherries and many soft fruits.

Cherries were brought to England by the Romans and both sweet and sour varieties have grown prolifically in Kent's moist soil ever since. The last 40 years have seen something of a decline in the number of cherry orchards, due to the highly labour intensive methods of harvesting involved.

PICK-YOUR-OWN CHERRIES AT: Crowhurst Farm, Crowhurst Lane, Borough Green, Sevenoaks, Kent
Telephone: 0732 882905
Most orchards are only open for picking for one week of the year, so it is worthwhile telephoning before visiting any cherry orchard. Crowhurst grows 19 different varieties of cherry in 15 glorious acres of orchard.

Plump juicy cherries from The Garden of England, where as many as 19 different varieties can be found

There has been no decline in Kent's apple growing, however. Bramley's Seedling and Cox's Orange Pippin were originally discovered and developed in the region and remain widely cultivated today.

The coasts of Hampshire, Kent and Sussex have always enjoyed busy fishing industries and Sussex, in particular, still lands reasonable quantities of bass, conger eel and red and grey mullet while Rye in Kent is justly proud of its Dover sole. Farmed Pacific oysters from Whitstable rival Colchester's in their abundance and quality. Other shellfish caught around the south-east coast include crab, cockles, shrimps, clams and whelks, while lobsters are potted in quantity from May to October.

BOTTERELL SEATRADES, Harbour Road, Rye Harbour, Rye, Kent
Telephone: 0797 222875
Wholesale only – please telephone to make appointment to visit. Situated in one of the richest fishing areas in Britain, Botterell Seatrades takes advantage of the wide variety of prime fish which is caught locally. Dover sole, turbot, bass and scallops are sold to hotels and restaurants throughout Kent and Sussex, while the mainstays of plaice and lemon sole are mostly sent to Billingsgate Market for distribution all over the UK.

The growing of hops in Kent has been of great importance for centuries. Although originally used as a vegetable, it was in the 16th century that hops became extensively used for brewing in the region. Kent's countryside is dotted with low cone-roofed buildings known as oast houses – most farmyards possess at least one.

Until quite recently, hop-picking holidays in Kent were akin to grape-picking holidays in France. Families and students would stay on hop farms during the summer, helping with the back-breaking harvesting while at the same time earning extra cash for the holidays.

Hop-picking holidays are rare today but it is still possible to wallow in nostalgia at various hop farms, some working and some as historical artefacts.

THE WHITBREAD HOP FARM, Beltring, Paddock Wood, Nr. Tonbridge
Telephone: 0622 872068
100 acres of hops, grown for the Whitbread breweries around the UK. Hop-picking is not permitted but visitors can watch everything that goes on, as well as seeing Shire horses, a trout lake and the hop museum.

MUSEUM OF KENT RURAL LIFE, Lock Lane, Sandling, Maidstone
Telephone: 0622 63936
A fascinating collection of exhibits of days gone by, including a small hop field, crops, a herb garden, an orchard, an apiary and a shop selling organic produce. There is a limited period when hops may be picked, during the Agricultural Show in September – telephone the museum for full details.

There are now over 1000 vineyards in England successfully cultivating a wide variety of grapes

VINES have been planted on the kinder slopes of England's green and pleasant land since Roman times. Many vineyards were cultivated by the monks and it was not until Henry VIII dissolved the monasteries in England that viticulture went into total decline.

Serious interest in the cultivation of vines in southern England was aroused during the 1940s, when it was rediscovered that south-facing slopes were sufficiently well-drained and protected to allow certain types of vine to flourish. The very first commercial enterprise was established at Hambledon Hall in Hampshire in 1952 by Sir Guy Salisbury-Jones.

Eventually, German grapes were grafted onto English-grown roots and proved successful, if carefully protected from the weather. There are currently over 1000 vineyards in England, concentrated largely in the warmer south-eastern counties, with Kent being by far the most prolific. The English Vineyard Association was established to promote the interests of the wine growers – its members are permitted to display the EVA Seal of Quality on their bottles.

VINEYARDS TO VISIT

THE THAMES VALLEY, Stanlake Park, Twyford, Reading, Berkshire
Telephone: 0734 340176
10.3 hectares of vines.
Open all year, tours available by appointment.
The vineyard, set in the grounds of a beautiful historic house and gardens, has its own winery with free tastings for visitors and a shop.

BEAULIEU, John Montagu Buildings, Beaulieu, Brockenhurst, Hampshire
Telephone: 0590 612345
2.5 hectares of vines.
Open in the summer only, tours available by appointment.
Set in the wonderful surroundings of historic Beaulieu, this smaller vineyard has its own shop selling estate bottled wines.

LAMBERHURST, Ridge Farm, Lamberhurst, Tonbridge Wells, Kent
Telephone: 0892 890286
20 hectares of vines.
Open all year, tours by appointment.
Probably one of Britain's most famous vineyards, Lamberhurst has its own winery with free tastings, a shop, a small restaurant and plenty of scope for country walks and picnics.

CARR TAYLOR, Yew Tree Farm, Westfield, Hastings, East Sussex
Telephone: 0424 752501
8.75 hectares of vines.
Open all year, tours by appointment.
Carr Taylor wines have gained an excellent reputation and the vineyard is well worth a visit. There is a winery, tasting opportunities, and a shop; refreshments can be arranged given prior notice.

Ancient watercress beds in Alresford, Hampshire

The village of Alresford in Hampshire houses one of England's oldest and most traditional food growing systems. In ancient stone beds, WATERCRESS seeds are fed by artesian springs which take their water from the North Downs. Contrary to popular belief, the watercress does not actually grow in the River Test itself, which flows gracefully through the village.

English watercress is available all year round and is discernable by its strong, peppery flavour. It appears in salads and as a garnish but can also be made into delicious summer soups and sauces.

Hampshire also gained such a reputation for its wide range of pork products that its inhabitants became known as Hampshire Hogs. It also used to benefit from the herds of wild pigs living in the New Forest. Attempts were made during Edwardian times to train the New Forest pigs to hunt for Britain's only wild truffles but no great successes were ever recorded. Hams and cold meats featured heavily in country houses and villages alike, with offal playing a much lesser role than in the rest of the country.

The lower lands of Hampshire, Berkshire, Surrey, Sussex and Kent enjoy good dairying conditions and many dairy farms are to be found in these counties.

JOHN STRANGE, 16 High Street, Lyndhurst, Hampshire
Telephone: 0703 283300
The John Strange company has been established as a game dealer for over 200 years, selling from the shop in Lyndhurst to local customers and now on a wholesale basis, too, to local caterers, restaurants and hotels.

Their speciality is wild venison from Hampshire's New Forest. During the venison season, as many as 100 deer per week are brought into the premises for skinning and cutting. As well as venison, John Strange also sell a wide range of locally shot game birds, such as pheasant, partridge, teal and mallard.

The shop is open from Wednesday to Saturday, 9.00 am to 5.00 pm.

---

there is also a thriving ice-cream and yoghurt making tradition, answering the call of London's restaurants, specialist food shops and delicatessens. Ice cream was popular with fashionable society early in the 19th century but it was not until the summer of 1850 that it was made available to the masses. Sold in parks and from barrows, it took some time to become firmly established as a popular summer treat.

EARL GREY ICE CREAM WITH HOT CARAMEL SAUCE

ICE CREAM

26 fl oz/750 ml/2½ cups double cream
18 fl oz/500 ml/1¾ cups milk
10 oz/300 g/1¼ cups sugar
4½ oz/125 g/½ cup Earl Grey tea

CARAMEL SAUCE

9 oz/250 g/1 cup caster sugar
9 fl oz/250 ml/1 cup double cream
1 oz/30 g/1 tbs honey

To make the ice cream, boil together 18 fl oz/500 ml/1¾ cups of double cream and the milk, sugar and tea. Leave to get cold and then pour through a sieve. Semi whip the remaining double cream and fold in the tea mixture. Churn in an ice cream machine or freeze in the freezer, stirring at hourly intervals, until set.

To make the caramel sauce, cook the sugar dry in a clean pan until golden in colour. Don't let the sugar get too dark or it will take on a bitter taste. Boil the cream with the honey, then add to the sugar. Cook the sauce to 150°C/300°F/Gas Mark 2, then leave to stand. Using an ice cream scoop arrange 3 balls of ice cream on a plate, and garnish with a sprig of mint. Pour the hot caramel sauce into a sauce boat and serve immediately.

Serves 4–6
(MICHAEL COAKER AT THE MAYFAIR HOTEL)

LOSELEY PARK HALL, Guildford, Surrey
Telephone: 0483 304440
As well as Loseley Hall itself, the estate boasts a farm and a farm-shop, where all the famous Loseley products may be purchased. These include a wide range of dairy products, such as ice-cream, yoghurt, cream and milk, organic bakery products and a new range of pork and hams. Visitors may visit the farm and see the organically-managed animals.
Opening times: 29 May to 28 September Wednesday, Thursday and Friday Saturday afternoons only

COW'S MILK CHEESES

D & G DOBLE, Castle Hill Farm, Rotherfield, Crowborough, Sussex
Telephone: 089 285 2207
• Castle Hill – unpasteurised, full-fat, hard

NEAL'S YARD CREAMERIES, 1 Home Farm Cottages, Everlands Estate, Sevenoaks, Kent
Telephone: 0732 461020
• Low-fat cheese – unpasteurised skimmed milk, soft, unsalted
• Wealdon Rounds – unpasteurised
• Fromage Blanc – creamy, unpasteurised, also available extra thick

VILLAGE MAID, Spencers Wood, Reading, Berkshire
Telephone: 0734 884564
• Wellington – full-fat, hard, unpasteurised

SHEEP'S MILK CHEESES

NEPICAR FARM, Wrotham Heath, Sevenoaks, Kent
Telephone: 0732 883040
• Carolina – unpasteurised hard, adapted from a Wensleydale recipe, matured for 2 months
• Cecilia – unpasteurised, hard, matured for 2 months

PUTLANDS FARM, Duddleswell, Uckfield, East Sussex
Telephone: 0825 712647
• Sussex Slipcote – full-fat, soft
• Duddleswell – hard, matured
• Feta

WIELD WOOD ESTATE, Alresford, Hampshire
Telephone: 0420 63151
• Walda – Gouda-style, unpasteurised, also available with peppercorns

GOAT'S MILK CHEESES

BATTLE ABBEY FARM, Powdermill Lane, Battle, East Sussex
• Battle Abbey – unpasteurised, soft, lactic curd
• Senlac – unpasteurised, adapted from Wensleydale recipe

BUNKER FARM, Basingstoke Road, Greenham Common South, Newbury, Berkshire
Telephone: 0635 45535
• Newbury – unpasteurised, full-fat, soft

NEAL'S YARD CREAMERIES – details as above
• Chevre – soft, creamy, unpasteurised, available in wheels or logs

WELLS STORES, Streatley, near Reading, Berkshire
Telephone: 0491 872367
Wells Stores, run by Britain's foremost cheese expert Patrick Rance and his son Hugh, sells a huge range of the country's finest cheeses.
Opening times: Monday to Saturday 9.30 am to 5.30 pm
Wednesday 9.30 am to 1.00 pm

The town of Aylesbury in Buckinghamshire has given its name to one of the region's most famous poultry dishes, AYLESBURY DUCK. This stems from the days when Aylesbury and the surrounding villages contained a large number of ponds which were home to ducks.

Brisk local trade in duck attracted other duck farmers from further afield until the area became recognised as a market-place for this particular type of poultry. Pure Aylesbury ducks are not widely bred today and most ducks found in the region are a hybrid of the Pekin duck.

In 1874, Sara Jane Cooper of the Angel Hotel in OXFORD made a thick, rich marmalade using fresh Seville oranges. It was so popular that her father, Frank Cooper, decided to sell it from his grocery in The High, specially packaged in attractive earthenware pots.

The only thing which has changed about Oxford Marmalade over the years is its availability. Frank Cooper's distinctively labelled marmalade, full of coarse cut orange peel in rich, dark jelly, is now sold through supermarkets and retail outlets across Britain and Europe.

The enormous student population of Oxford and the colleges have also given rise to many of their own dishes, often served with great pomp and circumstance at banquets and festivals. New College pudding and Halygog, two traditional college dishes, are still occasionally served today.

The town's butchers, too, formed associations with certain colleges, gaining valuable business by offering tailor-made services. In this way, the leg steak of lamb known as Oxford John became a college speciality, although its fame has now extended beyond Oxford. Brawn, made from pig's head, was also popular for afternoon tea.

In common with most student towns, Oxford has its fair share of renowned breweries, brewing beer specially designed for the academic palate. Even in these days of mass lager drinking, there is still a lively market for interesting real ales in Oxford.

Many of the pubs serve beers brewed by the independent Oxford brewery MORRELL'S who have made sure that their beers are closely associated with student life by naming them accordingly – Varsity, College and Graduate.

OXFORD PUBS SERVING MORRELL'S BEER
The Black Boy, 91 Old High Street, Headington
The Fir Tree Tavern, 163 Iffley Road
The Gardeners Arms, Plantation Road
The Globe, 59 Cranham Street, Jericho
Old Tom, 60 Western Road
The Prince of Wales, 80 Cowley Road

REFERENCE SECTION

FOOD FROM BRITAIN
301–344 Market Towers
New Covent Garden Market
London SW8 5NQ
Tel: 071 720 2144

ASPARAGUS GROWERS'
ASSOCIATION
133 Eastgate
Louth
Lincolnshire
Tel: 0507 602427

BRITISH CHARTER QUALITY
BACON
19 Cornwall Terrace
London NW1 4QP
Tel: 071 935 7980

BRITISH CHICKEN
INFORMATION SERVICE
Bury House
126–128 Cromwell Road
London SW7 4ET
Tel: 071 373 7757

BRITISH DEER FARMER'S
ASSOCIATION
Holly Lodge
Spencers Lane
Berkswell
Coventry CV7 7BZ
Tel: 0203 465957

BRITISH DUCK INFORMATION
SERVICE
Thames View House
6 St Peter's Road
Twickenham
Middlesex
Tel: 081 892 2720

BRITISH GOOSE PRODUCERS'
ASSOCIATION
c/o High Holborn House
High Holborn
London WC1V 6XS
Tel: 071 242 4683

BRITISH OAT & BARLEY
ASSOCIATION
6 Catherine Street
London WC2B 5JJ
Tel: 071 836 2460

BRITISH POULTRY
FEDERATION LTD
High Holborn House
High Holborn
London WC1V 6XS
Tel: 071 242 4683

BRITISH SUMMER FRUITS
ASSOCIATION
Sandbands
Graveney
Faversham
Kent ME13 9DJ
Tel: 0795 532728

BRITISH TOURIST AUTHORITY
Thames Tower
Blacks Road
London W6 9EL
Tel: 081 846 9000

BRITISH TROUT ASSOCIATION
14 Parkway
London NW1 7AN
Tel: 071 911 0313

BRITISH TURKEY
INFORMATION SERVICE
Bury House
126–128 Cromwell Road
London SW7 4ET
Tel: 071 244 7701

BUTTER INFORMATION
COUNCIL
Tubs Hill House
London Road
Sevenoaks
Kent TN13 1BL
Tel: 0732 460060

DELICATESSEN & FINE FOODS
ASSOCIATION
PO Box 4
Northreach
Cheltenham
CH54 3LN
Tel: 0285 720009

EAST LINCOLNSHIRE
GROWERS LTD
The Firs
London Road
Kirton
Boston
Lincolnshire PE20 1DS
Tel: 0205 722666

ENGLISH APPLES & PEARS LTD
80 Wincheap
Canterbury
Kent CT1 3RS
Tel: 0227 451663

ENGLISH VINEYARDS
ASSOCIATION
38 West Park
London SE9 4RH
Tel: 081 857 0452

FARMHOUSE ENGLISH CHEESE
BUREAU
PO Box 457
Wells
Somerset BA5 1UX
Tel: 0749 77953

FARM SHOP AND PICK-YOUR-
OWN ASSOCIATION
Agriculture House
Knightsbridge
London SW1X 7NJ
Tel: 071 235 5077

FLOUR ADVISORY BUREAU
21 Arlington Street
London SW1A 1RN
Tel: 071 493 2521

FRESH FRUIT & VEGETABLE
INFORMATION BUREAU
Bury House
126–128 Cromwell Road
London SW7 4ET
Tel: 071 373 7734

GREAT GRIMSBY – EUROPE'S
FOOD TOWN
Municipal Offices
Town Hall Square
Grimsby DN31 1HU
Tel: 0472 242000

HIGHLANDS AND ISLANDS
DEVELOPMENT BOARD
Bridge House
20 Bridge Street
Inverness IV1 1QR
Tel: 0463 234171

HOME GROWN CEREALS
AUTHORITY
Hamlyn House
Highgate Hill
London N19 5PR
Tel: 081 263 3391

INDUSTRIAL DEVELOPMENT
BOARD FOR NORTHERN
IRELAND
IDB House
64 Chichester Street
Belfast BT1 4JX
Tel: 0232 233233

LIVESTOCK MARKETING
COMMISSION FOR
NORTHERN IRELAND
57 Malone Road
Belfast BT9 6SA
Tel: 0232 381022

MALVERN CHEESEWRIGHTS
Bennett's Dairies & Farms Ltd.
Manor Farm
Lower Wick
Worcester WR2 4BT
Tel: 0905 748100

MEAT & LIVESTOCK
COMMISSION
PO Box 44
Winterhill House
Snowdon Road
Milton Keynes MK6 1AX
Tel: 0908 677577

MILK MARKETING BOARD OF
ENGLAND & WALES
Thames Ditton
Surrey KT7 0EL
Tel: 081 398 4101

MILK MARKETING BOARD FOR
NORTHERN IRELAND
456 Antrim Road
Belfast BT15 5GD
Tel: 0232 770123

MUSHROOM GROWERS'
ASSOCIATION
2 St Paul's Street
Stanford
Lincolnshire PE9 2BE
Tel: 0780 66888

NATIONAL ASSOCIATION OF
CIDER MAKERS
c/o The Taunton Cider Co Ltd.
Norton Fitzwarren
Taunton
Somerset TA2 6RD
Tel: 0823 283141

NATIONAL FARMERS' UNION
OF ENGLAND & WALES
Agriculture House
Knightsbridge
London SW1X 7NJ
Tel: 071 235 5077

NATIONAL FARMERS' UNION
OF SCOTLAND
17 Grosvenor Crescent
Edinburgh EH12 5EN
Tel: 031 337 4333

NATIONAL FEDERATION OF
FISHMONGERS LTD.
Pisces
London Road
Feering
Colchester
Essex CO5 9ED
Tel: 0376 571391

NATIONAL TRUST
36 Queen Anne's Gate
London SW1H 9AS
Tel: 071 222 9251

NORTH OF SCOTLAND MILK
MARKETING BOARD
Claymore Creamery
Balmikeith Industrial Estate
Forres Road
Nairn IV12 5QW
Tel: 0667 53344

OATS INFORMATION BUREAU
24–28 Bloomsbury Way
London SW1X 0NB
Tel: 071 589 4874

SCOTCH QUALITY BEEF &
LAMB ASSOCIATION
13th Avenue
Edinburgh Exhibition & Trade
Centre
Ingliston
Edinburgh EH28 8NB
Tel: 031 333 5335

SCOTCH WHISKY
ASSOCIATION
20 Atholl Crescent
Edinburgh EH3 8HF
Tel: 031 229 4883

SCOTTISH MILK MARKETING
BOARD
Underwood Road
Paisley
Renfrewshire PA3 1TJ
Tel: 041 887 1234

SCOTTISH SALMON
GROWERS' ASSOCIATION
Drummond House
Scott Street
Perth PH1 5EJ
Tel: 0738 35420

SCOTTISH SALMON
INFORMATION SERVICE
26 Fitzroy Square
London W1P 6BT
Tel: 071 388 7421

SCOTTISH SALMON SMOKERS'
ASSOCIATION
33 Melville Street
Edinburgh EH3 7JF
Tel: 031 220 2256

SEA FISH INDUSTRY
AUTHORITY
Sea Fisheries House
10 Young Street
Edinburgh EH2 4JQ
Tel: 031 225 2515

SHELLFISH ASSOCIATION OF
GREAT BRITAIN
Fishmongers' Hall
London Bridge
London EC4R 9EL
Tel: 071 283 8305

STILTON CHEESEMAKERS'
ASSOCIATION
PO Box 11
Buxton
Derbyshire SK17 6PR
Tel: 0298 26224

A TASTE OF ULSTER
River House
48 High Street
Belfast BT1 2DS
Tel: 0232 236600

THE TEA COUNCIL
Sir John Lyon House
5 High Timber Street
London EC4V 3NJ
Tel: 071 248 1024

ULSTER FARMERS' UNION
475–477 Antrim Road
Belfast BT15 3DA
Tel: 0232 370222

ULSTER FISH COMMITTEE
475–477 Antrim Road
Belfast BT15 3DA
Tel: 0232 370222

WOMEN'S FARMING UNION
Crundells
Matfield
Kent TN12 7EA
Tel: 0892 722803

HOTELS AND RESTAURANTS

SCOTLAND

Airds Hotel
Port Appin
Strathclyde
Tel: 063 173 236

Ardoe House
South Deeside Road
Aberdeen
Tel: 0224 867355

Ardsheal House
Kentallan
Appin
Strathclyde
Tel: 063 174 227

Buttery
652 Argyle Street
Glasgow
Strathclyde
Tel: 041 221 8188

Cellar Restaurant
24 East Green
Anstruther
Fife
Tel: 0333 310378

Champany Inn Restaurant
Champany
Lothian
Tel: 050 683 4532

Culloden House Hotel
Culloden
Inverness
Tel: 0463 790461

The Dower House
Muir of Ord
Highland
Tel: 0463 870090

The Howard
32 Great King Street
Nerth Lane
Edinburgh
Tel: 031 225 3106

Inverlochy Castle
Fort William
Inverness
Tel: 0397 2177/2188

Invery House
Bridge of Feugh
Banchory
Grampian
Tel: 03302 4782

Kinloch Lodge
Sleat
Isle of Skye
Tel: 04713 214

Kinlochbervie Hotel
Kinlochbervie
Highland
Tel: 097 182 275

Meldrum House Hotel
Oldmeldrum
Grampian
Tel: 06512 2294

October Restaurant
128 Drymen Road
Bearsden
Nr Glasgow
Strathclyde
Tel: 041 942 7272

One Devonshire Gardens
1 Devonshire Gardens
Glasgow
Strathclyde
Tel: 041 399 2001

Peat Inn
Nr Cupar
Fife
Tel: 033484 206

Prestonfield House
Priestfield Road
Edinburgh
Tel: 031 668 3346

Summer Isles Hotel
Achiltibuie
Nr Ullapool
Highland
Tel: 085 482 282

Tullich Lodge
Ballater
Grampian
Tel: 03397 55406

PUBS AND INNS

Aileen Chraggan Hotel
Weem
Nr Aberfeldy
Tayside
Tel: 0887 20346

Babbity Bowster
16 Blackfriars Street
Glasgow
Tel: 041 552 5055

Glenmoriston Arms
Invermoriston
Highland
Tel: 0320 51206

Kilberry Inn
Kilberry
Nr Tarbert
Strathclyde
Tel: 08803 223

NORTHERN IRELAND

The Ben Medigan Restaurant
Belfast Castle
Antrim Road
Belfast
Tel: 0232 776925

The Bushmills Inn
25 Main Street
Bushmills
Co. Antrim
Tel: 026 57 32339

The Dunadry Hotel
Dunadry
Co. Antrim
Tel: 08494 32474

The Gas Lamp
47 Court Street
Newtownards
Co. Down
Tel: 0247 811225

Hillside Restaurant
Main Street
Hillsborough
Co. Down
Tel: 0846 682 765

The Kiln Restaurant
Old Glenarm Road
Larne
Co. Antrim
Tel: 0574 60924

The Londonderry Arms Hotel
120 Harbour Road
Carnlough
Co. Antrim
Tel: 0574 885255

Old Inn
15 Main Street
Crawfordsburn
Co. Down
Tel: 0247 853255

The Old School House
Restaurant
100 Balleydrain Road
Comber
Co. Down
Tel: 0238 541182

The Portaferry Hotel
10 The Strand
Portaferry
Co. Down
Tel: 0247 728231

Ramore
The Harbour
Portrush
Co. Antrim
Tel: 0265 824313

Roscoff's
7 Lesley House
Shaftesbury Square
Belfast
Tel: 0232 331532

Woodlands
29 Spa Road
Ballynahinch
Co. Down
Tel: 0238 562650

COUNTRY (GUEST) HOUSES

The Beeches
10 Dunadry Road
Muckamore
Co. Antrim
Tel: 08494 33161

Grange Lodge
7 Grange Road
Dungannon
Co. Tyrone
Tel: 08687 84212

Greenacres Guest House
5 Manse Road
Newtownards
Co. Down
Tel: 0247 816193

MacDuff's Restaurant
Blackheath House
112 Killeague Road
Blackhill
Coleraine
Co. Londonderry
Tel: 0265 868433

PUBS AND INNS

Balloo House
Killinchy
Co. Down
Tel: 0238 541210

Brown Trout Inn
209 Agivey Road
Aghadowey
Co. Londonderry
Tel: 0265 868209

McCuaig's Bar
The Quay
Rathlin
Co. Antrim

O'Reilly's
7 Rathfriland Road
Dromara
Co. Down
Tel: 0238 532209

Plough Inn
The Square
Hillsborough
Co. Down
Tel: 0846 682985

WALES

Armless Dragon
97 Wyverne Road
Cathays
Cardiff
Tel: 0222 382 357

Beckfords
15 Upper Church Street
Chepstow
Gwent
Tel: 02912 6547

Bodysgallen Hall Hotel
Llandudno
Gwynedd
Tel: 0492 584466

Cemlyn
High Street
Harlech
Tel: 0874 754525

Conrah Country Hotel
Chancery
Aberystwyth
Dyfed
Tel: 0970 617 941

Fairyhill
Reynoldston
Nr Swansea
Tel: 0792 390139

The Great House
Laleston
Nr Bridgend
Mid Glamorgan
Tel: 0656 57644

Llangoed Hall
Llyswen
Brecon
Powys
Tel: 0874 754 525

Maes-Y-Neuadd
Talsarnau
Nr Harlech
Gwynedd
Tel: 0766 780200

Ye Olde Bulls Head Inn
Castle Street
Beaumaris
Anglesey
Gwynedd
Tel: 0248 810329

Plas Bodegroes
Nefyn Road
Pwllheli
Gwynedd
Tel: 0758 612363

Quayles
8 Romilly Crescent
Canton
Cardiff
Tel: 0222 341264

Richard Wilson Arts Centre
Baladeulyn
Nantlle
Caernarfon
Gwynedd
Tel: 0286 880676

The Walnut Tree
Llandewi Skirrid
Nr Abergavenny
Gwent
Tel: 0873 2797

PUBS AND INNS

Bush Inn
Llandissilio
Nr Clynderwen
Dyfed
Tel: 09916 626

Griffin Inn
Llyswen
Nr Brecon
Powys
Tel: 087 485 241

The Queen's Head
Glanwydden
Gwynedd
Tel: 0492 46570

NORTHERN ENGLAND

Betty's Cafe and Tearoom
1 Parliament Street
Harrogate
N. Yorkshire
Tel: 0423 502 746

The Box Tree
29 Church Street
Ilkley
W. Yorkshire
Tel: 0743 608484

Farlam Hall
Brampton
Cumbria
Tel: 06976 234

Fishermans Lodge
Jesmond Drive
Jesmond
Newcastle Upon Tyne
Tyne & Wear
Tel: 091 261 7356

The Market Restaurant
104 High Street
Smithfield City Centre
Manchester
Tel: 061 834 3743

Middlethorpe Hall Hotel
Bishopthorpe Road
York
Tel: 0904 641241

Miller Howe
Rayrigge Road
Windermere
Cumbria
Tel: 09662 2536

Mount Royal Hotel
The Mount
York
Tel: 0904 628856

Northcote Manor
Northcote Road
Langho
Lancashire
Tel: 0254 240555

Paul Heathcote's
101/106 Higher Road
Longridge
Preston
Lancashire
Tel: 0772 784 969

Restaurant Nineteen
19 North Park Road
Heaton
Bradford
West Yorkshire
Tel: 0274 492559

Sharrow Bay Hotel
Ullswater
Penrith
Cumbria
Tel: 07684 86301

PUBS AND INNS

Black Bull Inn
Moulton
Nr Richmond
N. Yorkshire
Tel: 032 577289

Malt Shovel Inn
Oswaldkirk
Nr Hemsley
N. Yorkshire
Tel: 04393 461

Masons Arms
Strawberry Bank
Nr Grange-over-Sands
Cumbria
Tel: 044 88 486

Milecastle Inn
Old Military Road
Haltwhistle
Northumberland
Tel: 0498 20682

Pheasant Inn
Bassenthwaite
Nr Cockermouth
Cumbria
Tel: 059 681 234

Royal Oak Inn
Bongate
Appleby
Cumbria
Tel: 0930 51463

String of Horses
Heads Nook
Faugh
Carlisle
Tel: 022 870 297

Three Acres Inn
Royal House
Nr Huddersfield
W. Yorkshire
Tel: 0484 602606

Warenford Lodge
Warenford
Nr Belford
Northumberland
Tel: 066 83 453

Wasdale Head Inn
Wasdale
Nr Gosforth
Cumbria
Tel: 094 06 229

THE MIDLANDS

The Beetle and Wedge Hotel
Ferry Lane
Moulsford on Thames, Oxon
Tel: 0491 651381

The Belfry Hotel
Handforth
Wilmslow, Cheshire
Tel: 061 437 0511

The Bucklemaker
30 Mary Ann Street
St Pauls Square
Birmingham
Tel: 021 200 2515

Calcot Manor
Tetbury
Nr Beverston, Glos
Tel: 066 689 391

Crabwell Manor
Parkgate Road
Mollington
Chester
Tel: 0244 851 666

The Elms Hotel
Stockton Road
Abberley
Nr Worcester
Tel: 0299 896666

The Feathers
Bull Ring
Ludlow, Salop
Tel: 0584 875261

Fossebridge Inn
Fossebridge
Northleach, Glos
Tel: 0285 720721

The George
71 St Martin
Stamford, Lincs
Tel: 0780 55171

Grafton Manor
Grafton Lane
Bromsgrove, H & W
Tel: 0527 579007

The Greenway Hotel
Shurdington
Cheltenham, Glos
Tel: 0242 862352

Hope End
Hope End
Ledbury, H & W
Tel: 0531 3613

The Lygon Arms
Broadway, Worcs
Tel: 0386 852255

Mallory Court
Harbury Lane
Bishop's Tachbrook
Leamington Spa, Warwicks
Tel: 0926 330 21

Le Manoir Aux Quat' Saisons
Church Road
Great Milton, Oxon
Tel: 0844 278881

15 North Parade
off Banbury Road
Oxford
Tel: 0865 513773

Norton Place Hotel
180 Lifford Lane
Kings Norton
Birmingham
Tel: 021 433 5656

Nuthurst Grange
Nuthurst Grange Lane
Hockley Heath, W. Midlands
Tel: 05643 3972

Old Post Office
9 The Square
Clun, Salop
Tel: 05884 687

Plough and Harrow Hotel
135 Hagley Road
Edgbaston
Birmingham
Tel: 021 454 4111

The Stanneylands Hotel
Stanneylands Road
Wilmslow, Cheshire
Tel: 0625 525225

The Whipper Inn Hotel
The Market Place
Oakham, Leics
Tel: 0572 756971

PUBS AND INNS

Bird in Hand
Knoll Green
Mobberley
Cheshire
Tel: 0565 873149

Butchers Arms
Woolhope
Nr Hereford
Tel: 043 277 281

Dun Cow
Chelford Road
Ollerton
Cheshire
Tel: 0565 3093

Hobnails Inn
Little Washbourne
Nr Tewkesbury
Gloucestershire
Tel: 024 262 237

Lambs Inn
High Street
Shipton Under Wychwood
Oxfordshire
Tel: 0993 830 465

Mason's Arms
Wilmcote
Nr Stratford-Upon-Avon
Warwickshire
Tel: 0789 297 416

Roebuck
Brimfield
Nr Ludlow
Shropshire
Tel: 058 472 230

Sir Charles Napier
Sprigs Holly
Chinnor
Oxfordshire
Tel: 024 026 3011

Snitterfield Arms
Snitterfield
Nr Stratford-Upon-Avon
Tel: 0789 731294

EAST ANGLIA

Adlard's
79 Upper St Giles Street
Norwich
Tel: 0603 633522

The Angel Hotel
Angel Hill
Bury St Edmunds, Suffolk
Tel: 0284 753926

Beehive
The Street
Horringer
Suffolk
Tel: 028 488 260

Congham Hall
Lynn Road
Grimston
Kings Lynn, Norfolk
Tel: 0485 600250

The Crown
90 High Street
Southwold, Suffolk
Tel: 0502 722275

Hintlesham Hall
Hintlesham
Ipswich
Tel: 047 387 334

Marlborough Head
Mill Lane
Dedham
Essex
Tel: 0206 323124

Midsummer House
Midsummer Common
Cambridge
Tel: 0223 69299

Oaksmere
Brome
Nr Eye
Suffolk
Tel: 0379 870326

Old Bridge Hotel
1 High Street
Huntingdon, Cambs
Tel: 0480 52681

The Old Fire Engine House
25 St Mary's Street
Ely, Cambs
Tel: 0353 662582

The Old Rectory
103 Yarmouth Road
Thorpe St Andrew
Norwich
Tel: 0603 39357

Pier at Harwich
The Quay
Harwich, Essex
Tel: 0255 241212

Seafood Restaurant
85 North Quay
Great Yarmouth, Norfolk
Tel: 0493 856009

Seckford Hall Hotel
Woodbridge, Suffolk
Tel: 0394 385678

Starr Restaurant
Market Place
Great Dunmow, Essex
Tel: 0377 874321

Le Talbooth and Maison Talbooth
Cunhill
Dedham
Nr Colchester, Essex
Tel: 0206 323150

PUBS AND INNS

Beehive
The Street
Horringer
Suffolk
Tel: 028 488 260

The Bell
Great North Road
Stilton
Cambridgeshire
Tel: 0733 241 066

Chequers Inn
High Street
Fowlmere
Nr Royston
Cambridgeshire
Tel: 076 382 369

Eight Bells
Bridge Street
Saffron Walden
Essex
Tel: 0799 22790

Free Press
7 Prospect Row
Cambridge
Tel: 0223 68337

Hare Arms
Stow Bardolph
Kings Lynn
Norfolk
Tel: 0366 382229

Oaksmere
Brome
Nr Eye
Suffolk
Tel: 0379 870326

The Ratcatchers' Inn
Cawston, Diss
Norfolk
Tel: 0603 871430

WEST OF ENGLAND

Beechfield House
Beanacre
Nr Melksham, Wilts
Tel: 0225 703700

Bishopstrow House
Bishopstrow
Warminster, Wilts
Tel: 0985 212312

The Castle Hotel
Castle Green
Tauntonm, Somerset
Tel: 0823 72671

Chedington Court Hotel
Chedington
Nr Beominster, Wilts
Tel: 0935 898265

Danescombe Valley Hotel
Lower Kelly
Calstock, Cornwall
Tel: 0822 832414

Gidleigh Park Hotel
Chagford, Devon
Tel: 064 73 2367

Halmpstone Manor
Bishops Tawton
Nr Barnstaple, Devon
Tel: 0271 830321

Huntstrete House
Huntstrete
Chelwood
Nr Bristol
Tel: 0761 490490

Langley House Hotel and
Restaurant
Langley Marsh
Wiveliscombe
Nr Taunton, Somerset
Tel: 0984 23318

Lower Pitt Restaurant
Lower Pitt
East Buckland
Barnstaple, Devon
Tel: 059 86 243

Lucknam Park
Colerne, Wilts
Tel: 0225 742777

Luttrell Arms
High Street
Dunster
Nr Minehead, Somerset
Tel: 0643 821555

Markwick & Hunt
129 Hotwell Road
Bristol
Tel: 0272 262658

Mortons House Hotel
East Street
Corfe Castle, Dorset
Tel: 0929 480988

Mr Bistro
East Quay
Mevagissey, Cornwall
Tel: 0726 842432

Nansidwell Country House
Mawnan Smith
Nr Falmouth, Cornwall
Tel: 0326 250340

Plumber Manor Restaurant
Hazelbury Bryan
Sturminster Newton, Wilts
Tel: 0258 72507

Popjoy's
Beau Nash's House
Sawclose
Bath
Tel: 0225 460494

The Priory Hotel
Western Road
Bath
Tel: 0225 331922

Royal Bath Hotel
Bath Road
Bournemouth, Dorset
Tel: 0202 555555

The Royal Crescent Hotel
16 Royal Crescent
Bath
Tel: 0225 319090

The Seafood Restaurant
Riverside
Padstow, Cornwall
Tel: 0841 532485

Sheldon Manor
Nr Chippenham, Wilts
Tel: 0249 653120

Summer Lodge
Eveshot
Dorchester, Dorset
Tel: 0935 83424

The Well House
St Keyne
Liskeard, Cornwall
Tel: 0579 42001

Whitechapel Manor
South Molton, Devon
Tel: 076 95 3377

Whitehouse Hotel and
Restaurant
Williton, Somerset
Tel: 0984 32306

White's Restaurant
93 High Street
Cricklade
Nr Swindon, Wilts
Tel: 0973 751110

PUBS AND INNS

George Hotel
4 South Street
Bridport, Dorset
Tel: 0308 23187

Greyhound Inn
Staple Fitzpaine
Nr Taunton
Somerset
Tel: 0823 480227

Nobody Inn
Doddiscombsleigh
Nr Exeter
Devon
Tel: 0647 52394

Rose and Crown
Trent
Nr Sherborne
Dorset
Tel: 0935 850776

Silver Plough
Pitton
Nr Salisbury
Wiltshire
Tel: 072 272 266

LONDON AND THE SOUTH EAST

LONDON

(Hotels and restaurants with
talented chefs using fine
British ingredients)

HOTELS

Browns Hotel
Albemarle Street
London W1
Tel: 071 493 6020

The Capital Hotel
22–24 Basil Street
Knightsbridge
London SW3
Tel: 071 589 5171

The Connaught Hotel
Carlos Place
London W1
Tel: 071 499 7070

The Halkin Hotel
Halkin Street
London SW1
Tel: 071 823 1033

The Hampshire Hotel
Leicester Square
London WC2
Tel: 071 839 9399

The Lanesborough Hotel
1 Lanesborough Place
London SW1
Tel: 071 259 5606

The May Fair Inter-Continental
Stratton Street
London W1
Tel: 071 629 7777

The Portman Inter-Continental
Truffles Restaurant
22 Portman Square
London W1
Tel: 071 486 5844

The Savoy
Strand
London WC2
Tel: 071 836 4343

RESTAURANTS

Chesham's
The Sheraton Hotel, Belgravia
Pont Street
London SW1
Tel: 071 245 9273

Eatons
49 Elizabeth Street
London SW1
Tel: 071 730 0076

The English Garden
10 Lincoln Street
London SW3
Tel: 071 584 7292

The English House
3 Milner Street
London SW3
Tel: 071 584 3002

Foxtrot Oscar
79 Royal Hospital Road
London SW3
Tel: 071 352 7179

The Greenhouse
27a Hay's Mews
London W1
Tel: 071 499 3331

Harvey's
2 Bellevue Road
London SW17
Tel: 081 672 0114

Martin's
239 Baker Street
London NW1
Tel: 071 935 3130

Mosimann's
11b West Halkin Street
Belgrave Square
London SW1
Tel: 071 235 9625

One Ninety Queen's Gate
190 Queen's Gate
London SW7
Tel: 071 581 5666

Pomegranates
94 Grosvenor Road
London SW1
Tel: 071 828 6560

Simpson's-in-the-Strand
100 Piccadilly
London W1
Tel: 071 734 2002

Steph's Restaurant
39 Dean Street
London W1
Tel: 071 734 5976

Turner's
87–89 Walton Street
London SW3
Tel: 071 584 6711

PUBS AND INNS

Admiral Codrington
17 Mossop Street
London SW3
Tel: 071 589 4603

Alma
499 Old York Road
London SW18
Tel: 081 870 2537

Cock Tavern
Poultry Avenue
Central Markets
London EC1
Tel: 071 248 2918

Lamb and Flag
33 Rose Street
London WC2
Tel: 071 836 4108

Swan Tavern
66 Bayswater Road
London WC2
Tel: 071 262 5204

White Horse
1 Parsons Green
London SW6
Tel: 071 736 2115

SOUTH-EAST

The Bell Inn
Aston Clinton, Bucks
Tel: 0296 630252

Chewton Glen
Christchurch Road
New Milton, Hants
Tel: 0425 275341

Cisswood House
Sandy Gate Lane
Lower Beeding
Nr Horsham, E. Sussex
Tel: 0403 891216

Eastwell Manor
Eastwell Park
Boughton Aluph
Ashford, Kent
Tel: 0233 635751

Esseborne Manor
Hurstbourne Tarrant
Nr Andover, Hants
Tel: 026 476 444

Gravetye Manor
Vowels Lane
East Grinstead, W. Sussex
Tel: 0342 810567

Horsted Place
Little Horsted
Uckfield, E. Sussex
Tel: 082 575 581

The Hungry Monk Restaurant
The Street
Jevington
Nr Polegate, E. Sussex
Tel: 032 122178

Little Thakeham
Merrywood Lane
Storrington, W. Sussex
Tel: 0903 744416

Oakley Court Hotel
Windsor Road
Water Oakley
Nr Windsor, Bucks
Tel: 0628 74141

Ye Olde Bell Hotel
High Street
Hurley
Nr Maidenhead, Bucks
Tel: 062 822 5881

Old Manor House Restaurant
21 Palmerston Street
Romsey, Hants
Tel: 0794 517353

Partners West Street
2–4 West Street
Dorking, Surrey
Tel: 0306 882 826

Royal Oak Hotel
The Square
Yattendon
Nr Newbury, Bucks
Tel: 0635 201325

Topps Hotel
17 Regency Square
Brighton, E. Sussex
Tel: 0273 729334

Woods
Headley Road
Grayshott
Nr Hindhead, Surrey
Tel: 042 873 5555

PUBS AND INNS

Crowns
Haslemere
Weyhill
Surrey
Tel: 0428 3112

Fullers Arms
Oxley Green
Brightling
Nr Robertsbridge
East Sussex
Tel: 042 482 212

Harrow
East Ilsley
Nr Newbury
Berks
Tel: 063 528260

The Plough
Ivy Hatch
Nr Sevenoaks
Kent
Tel: 0732 810268

Three Lions
Stuckton Road
Stuckton
Fordingbridge
Hants
Tel: 0425 52489

Wykeham Arms
75 Kingsgate Street
Winchester
Hampshire
Tel: 0962 53834

Index

RECIPE INDEX